The U.S. Financial System in 2011:
How Will Sufficient Credit Be Provided?

Susan Hickok and Daniel E. Nolle

Office of the Comptroller of the Currency

OCC Economics Working Paper 2009-6

November 2009

Keywords: Bank Lending, Financial Crisis, Mortgage Market, Consumer Credit, Government Sponsored Enterprises JEL Classifications: G21, G01

The opinions in this paper are those of the authors and do not necessarily reflect those of the Office of the Comptroller of the Currency or the U.S. Treasury Department. The authors thank Mark Levonian, Nancy Wentzler, David Nebhut, Gary Whalen, and seminar participants at the Office of the Comptroller of the Currency for helpful comments, and Lily Chin, Amy Millen, and Rebecca Miller for editorial assistance.

The U.S. Financial System in 2011:
How Will Sufficient Credit Be Provided?

Susan Hickok and Daniel E. Nolle

Office of the Comptroller of the Currency

November 2009

Abstract

This paper uses *Flow of Funds* data on the level of net new credit extension to construct a bird's-eye view of what the financial market landscape might look like once the turmoil subsides and the economy has begun to recover. The paper targets two related questions: (1) How much credit must be extended in order to return the economy to its long-run trend growth? (2) What roles will the major credit providers likely play in that process? The mix of sources supplying credit for the home mortgage, consumer, and nonfinancial business sector markets is different, and so we consider each of those markets separately. We focus on the roles of banks, traditional nonbank credit providers (such as finance companies and pension funds), the corporate bond and commercial paper markets, and structured finance, including government-sponsored enterprise (GSE) mortgage-backed securities (MBS) issuance, consumer (i.e., nonmortgage) asset-backed securities (ABS) issuance, and the commercial mortgage-backed securities (CMBS) market.

As a reasonable assumption as to how the credit market may develop we start by positing a "baseline" scenario under which banks return to their long-run trend level of financing for home mortgage, consumer, and business sector borrowing. We then examine the extent to which other major providers of credit are likely to fill the remaining demand for credit. We consider what would happen if various of these credit providers were unable to meet the credit supply role asked of them in order to fulfill credit demand. We conclude that the revival of structured finance is crucial for home mortgage, consumer, and business sector credit provision if sharp adjustments in the cost of credit and major structural adjustments in credit markets are to be avoided. Specifically: (1) in the home mortgage market, GSE's sales of MBS sufficient to support about half of borrowers' credit needs are required for banks and private-label securitizers to operate at normal levels; and at least a modest role for private label MBS issuance is probably necessary to ensure adequate mortgage credit availability at a normal interest cost, (2) for consumer borrowing, without a substantial revival of the ABS market, banks and nonbank credit providers would not likely make up for the resultant shortfall without a sharp rise in the cost of consumer credit, and (3) for business sector credit, the re-emergence of the CMBS market is likely essential for adequate provision of commercial mortgage credit since, in the absence of large changes in the price of credit, banks are unlikely to make up for a large shortfall of CMBS-supported business sector credit extension. In contrast, banks and other credit channels likely would replace a credit shortfall resulting from a moribund commercial paper market without an undue rise in the cost of business credit.

I. Introduction

Policymakers and financial market participants are currently grappling with the issue of stabilizing banking and broader financial markets.[1] The dimensions of this problem are widely acknowledged to be without historical precedent, and public concern is correspondingly high. Hopes — and intentions — are focused on a "softer," purposely engineered, return to financial stability as opposed to a "hard landing." Understandably, given the situation's urgency, relatively little attention has been focused on the nature of the system after the dust settles. In the face of that gap, this study considers two related questions: (1) "How much credit will likely be demanded when the economy returns to its long-run trend growth?" (2) "What roles will the major credit providers likely play in fulfilling that demand?"

We focus on the economy-wide nature of the demand for and supply of credit in 2011, when many analysts and market observers expect a measure of stability to have returned to financial markets. Demand for credit comes from the private sector (both households and businesses) and from government; our focus is on the private sector.[2] For the household sector, we look at home mortgage borrowing and consumer (nonmortgage) borrowing in separate sections. For the (nonfinancial) business sector, we look at borrowing overall, and then separately consider business mortgage-related borrowing and nonmortgage business sector borrowing. Major providers of credit include banks (commercial banks and thrifts), significant nonbanks (e.g., finance companies and pension funds), private financial markets (corporate bond and commercial paper markets), and markets for securitized assets (government-sponsored

---

[1] See for example the Treasury Department's recent "white paper" on overhauling financial system regulation and supervision (Treasury Department (2009)), the U.S. Government Accountability Office (2009) report on the role of overleveraging in the current crisis, and the Bank for International Settlement (2009) *Annual Report*, detailing both the causes and recommended policy responses to the current crisis.

[2] We assume that federal government credit demand, as projected by the Congressional Budget Office (2009), can be readily met by traditional sources (most notably, foreign purchases of Treasury securities) and thus does not affect our analysis of private sector credit dynamics.

enterprise [GSE] issuance of mortgage-backed securities [MBS], private-label MBS issuers, commercial mortgage-backed securities issuance [CMBS], and consumer-loan asset-backed securities [ABS]).

Our perspective is, first, to look at historical patterns in the flow of credit for home mortgage, consumer, and business borrowing and to use these patterns to project the likely level of credit demand. Two key assumptions we employ are, first, that there are no major changes in credit costs, and second, that long-run equilibrium in the financial system is represented by a tendency on the part of major credit providers to maintain their traditional shares of credit extension. We rely heavily on long-run average behavior in our analysis, when this behavior appears stable, based on the argument that this behavior developed for a reason. Credit demand, for instance, will be split between home mortgage, consumer credit, and business credit needs. If this split remains fairly stable, as we will argue it does, we deem it reasonable to expect it to stay stable. If credit providers, such as banks, split up their credit extensions in a fairly stable manner for diversification benefits, we deem it reasonable to assume that they will continue to follow this credit extension pattern. Using this framework, we consider the extent to which the major providers of credit are likely to participate in financing consistent with the projected demand for credit. We specifically focus on whether the major credit extension sectors will be able to supply their traditional shares of credit to households and business. If that appears doubtful, we examine areas in which specific stress points or credit provision "bottlenecks" may emerge.

Our baseline scenario describes a return to moderate, long-run trend-type growth in the provision of bank credit, a development that is absolutely necessary for economic recovery. However, even if banks resume their long-run pattern of credit provision, this by itself would not generate sufficient new credit to meet likely demand if the economy returned to the normal trend level of gross domestic product (GDP) in 2011. Under these circumstances, we find that structured finance must experience a healthy revival not only in the mortgage market (primarily in the form of GSE MBS), but also in the reemergence of the consumer ABS market and the CMBS market to shares roughly equal to pre-bubble credit provision. We base this finding on analysis of various scenarios under which there is a too-anemic recovery of structured finance in home mortgage, consumer, and business credit markets. In such circumstances we consider whether banks and other providers might be able to "take up the slack." We conclude that unless there were a sharp adjustment in credit cost in the sector where structured finance did not revive, the banks and other providers would not likely fill the gap. Consequently, a moribund structured finance market is likely to lead to a serious brake on credit supply to the relevant borrowing sector.

The paper is organized as follows: section II includes a background discussion and describes our basic analytic approach. Section III considers possible roles for home mortgage market credit providers, highlighting in particular the consequences of different contribution rates from the GSEs. Section IV looks at different future scenarios for consumer credit provision. Section V explains different possible combinations of credit provision for the business sector. Finally, we summarize our analysis and consider several significant policy implications in section VI.

II. Background and Analytic Approach

Credit extension is intimately interlinked with economic growth, both as cause and effect.[3] In particular, the flow of new credit (rather than the outstanding balance of debt) is a

---

[3] A large literature has established a strong positive correlation between finance and economic growth, but the nature of the causal link is still under debate. See Levine (2005) for an overview.

major driver of economic growth. The Federal Reserve System's *Flow of Funds* details myriad dimensions of the flow of credit and the macroeconomy. This paper centers on the following credit flows: (1) net new home mortgage borrowing; (2) net new consumer borrowing (i.e., nonmortgage-related borrowing by households); and (3) net new nonfinancial businesses' borrowing.[4] The measure of economic output we use is nominal gross domestic product (GDP). We compare the net new flow of credit to the level of nominal GDP since GDP itself is a flow measurement.[5]

Table 1 focuses on the exact credit extension-to-GDP relationships in which we are interested. As a first step in the analysis, we compared the ratio of annual home mortgage,

Table 1. Long-Run Averages of Credit Extension-to-Nominal GDP: Home Mortgage, Consumer, and Business Borrowing				
Time Period	Net New Home Mortgage Borrowing as Percent of Nominal GDP	Net New Consumer Borrowing as Percent of Nominal GDP	Net New Nonfinancial Business Borrowing as Percent of Nominal GDP	Net New Nonfinancial Business Mortgage Borrowing as Percent of Nominal GDP
1971-2000	3.4	1.1	5.2	1.0
1983-2000	3.6	1.1	4.7	0.9
1992-2000	3.2	1.3	4.2	0.4
Parameters Used in Projections	3.4	1.2	4.5	0.8
Sources: *Flow of Funds*, Federal Reserve System; Haver Analytics.				

---

[4] As explained in section V, we examine business sector mortgage borrowing separately, and hence include its ratio in Table 1.

[5] Note that this juxtaposition of credit flow to GDP indicates that there should be no change in the level of credit flow when there is no change in GDP. Intuitively, if the same number of houses is built this year as last, resulting in no change in construction's contribution to GDP, we would expect there to be the same level of new mortgage credit flow this year as last year.

consumer, and business borrowing to GDP across three different, but overlapping, long-run time periods, representing three "takes" on the long-run relationship between private sector credit extension (and private sector borrowing) and economic output. Each of the periods ends in 2000, ahead of the housing market boom-and-bust; each incorporates at least one full business cycle as well. Table 1 generates the inputs for our analytic process. Broadly speaking, regardless of the length of the long-run period, the ratios of the four categories of credit extension to GDP appear to be relatively stable.[6] There is, therefore, justification for using a single (approximate) "average" long-run ratio, as indicated in the bottom row of Table 1.[7] Dollar values for each category of credit extension relative to the level of GDP are then derived from these, as Table 2 illustrates.

Table 2 outlines the underlying parameters of the quantitative starting point for our analysis.[8] The year-end 2008 Blue Chip consensus forecast of nominal GDP growth for 2009 combined with the assumption of 5 ½ percent annual nominal growth in 2010-2011 puts projected GDP at $16 trillion by 2011.[9] That figure, together with the Table 1 long-run average

---

[6] The ratio of each credit category to nominal GDP varies during different years in the business cycle. Because we are interested in equilibrium credit demand across the cycle, we use the average ratio for each type of credit, which is remarkably stable across the various business cycles.

[7] The ratios listed in the bottom row of Table 1 as "parameters used in projections" are averages of the three time-period average ratios, adjusted judgmentally. Net business borrowing was adjusted slightly down to give some weight to its declining trend over the three business cycles, resulting in a $30 billion lower target than would otherwise be the case. However, net business mortgage borrowing was adjusted a hair higher to give some weight to the observation that the most recent cycle looked unusually low relative to the two previous cycles, resulting in a $15 billion higher target.

[8] Box 1 at the end of this paper provides additional perspective to our analysis, giving background information on 1) long-run changes in the credit provision roles of banks, structured finance, and nonbanks; and 2) the nature of major credit provision "holes" into which the economy stumbled as the financial crisis unfolded. Of particular importance are the MBS market, the consumer ABS market, and the CMBS market.

[9] The Blue Chip consensus reports the average GDP forecast of over 50 forecasters. At end 2008 the consensus was projecting slightly under 1 percent nominal GDP growth for 2009. For 2010 and 2011 we assume 5 ½ percent growth because that is what nominal growth has averaged since 1985, after the high inflation years of the 1970s and early 1980s. If growth in any of these years comes in below these forecasted levels, then our analysis would be pushed out into 2012 but our conclusions would not change. Basically we are projecting what credit demand and

borrowing-to-nominal GDP ratios for home mortgage, consumer, and business borrowing, allows us to calculate the dollar amount of borrowing necessary to undergird economic output in 2011. Specifically, net new home mortgage borrowing, at 3.4 percent of the $16 trillion GDP, would be $550 billion; net new consumer borrowing, at 1.2 percent of 2011 nominal GDP,

Table 2. Schematic Parameters: Financial Market in 2011[a]		
Element	**Projected Level (billion)**	**Underlying Assumptions**
GDP	$16,000	Blue Chip nominal GDP forecast for 2009, plus assumption of nominal GDP growth rate of 5.5 percent in 2010 and again in 2011.
Net New Credit Extension:		
Home Mortgages	$550	Net new home mortgage borrowing at 3.4 percent of nominal GDP (see bottom row in Table 1)
Consumer Borrowing (nonmortgage)	$190	Net new consumer borrowing at 1.2 percent of nominal GDP (see bottom row in Table 1)
Business Borrowing (Total)	$720	Net new nonfinancial business borrowing at 4.5 percent of nominal GDP (see bottom row in Table 1)
Of which: **Business Mortgage Borrowing** (Commercial Real Estate Borrowing)	$125	Net new nonfinancial business mortgage borrowing at 0.8 percent of nominal GDP (see bottom row in Table 1)
[a] Calculations rounded to nearest $5 billion.		

would be $190 billion; total (mortgage-related and nonmortgage) nonfinancial business sector borrowing, at 4.5 percent of nominal GDP, would be $720 billion, of which mortgage-related business sector borrowing would be $125 billion.[10]

---

supply will look like once GDP reaches a certain level; the validity of our argument does not hinge on the precise timing of when this occurs.

[10] Financial projections are generally rounded to the nearest $5 billion in this paper; note also that ratios and projected levels are rounded independently, consistent with our goal of identifying broad trends rather than providing point estimates.

The third underlying element for our analysis is the role of the banking sector in credit provision, within the *Flow of Funds* context. We define the term "bank" to include both commercial banks and thrifts. Primarily this is a reflection of a new reality in banking after two of the largest thrifts, Washington Mutual and Countrywide, were merged into two large commercial banks as part of the Treasury Department– and Federal Reserve–led rescue efforts in mid-to-late 2008. In addition, many of the historic differences in scope of activities and business models that distinguished the two types of depository institutions from each other disappeared over the past decade. We exclude traditional broker-dealers from our analysis, however (even if they have converted to bank holding companies or been taken over by bank holding companies); broadly speaking, these firms have traditionally followed a different business model that does not supply substantial credit to ultimate borrowers in the economy, and we do not choose to speculate about potentially different future roles for these firms.

To gauge the credit role banks could reasonably be expected to fulfill we first consider the pattern of bank balance sheet growth. Figure 1 shows the pattern of net new acquisition of assets by the banking industry through 2008 (the darkest bar represents first half 2008 activity at an annualized pace).[11] To gauge what the future may look like, we estimate for the year 2011 what net asset aquisition would amount to for banks if their net new credit extension remained at its first-half 2008 ratio to nominal GDP.[12] That level of net new asset aquisition by banks for 2011 is shown by the lighter gray bar in Figure 1.[13]

---

[11] For 2008, we use the average annualized level of net new asset aquisition by banks for the first two quarters only under the reasoning that the extraordinary growth in two categories of net asset aquisition in the second half of 2008 were one-off, or at least very short-term, developments that do not reflect underlying credit extension strategies or patterns for the industry. The biggest single extraordinary net asset aquisition category in the second half of 2008 was the increase in reserves held at the Federal Reserve, to $753 billion, from traditionally low, almost trivial levels.

[12] The relationship between bank net new acquisition of financial assets and nominal GDP growth is very erratic. Under such circumstances, we make the assumption that the ratio of bank net new asset aquisition to nominal GDP

8

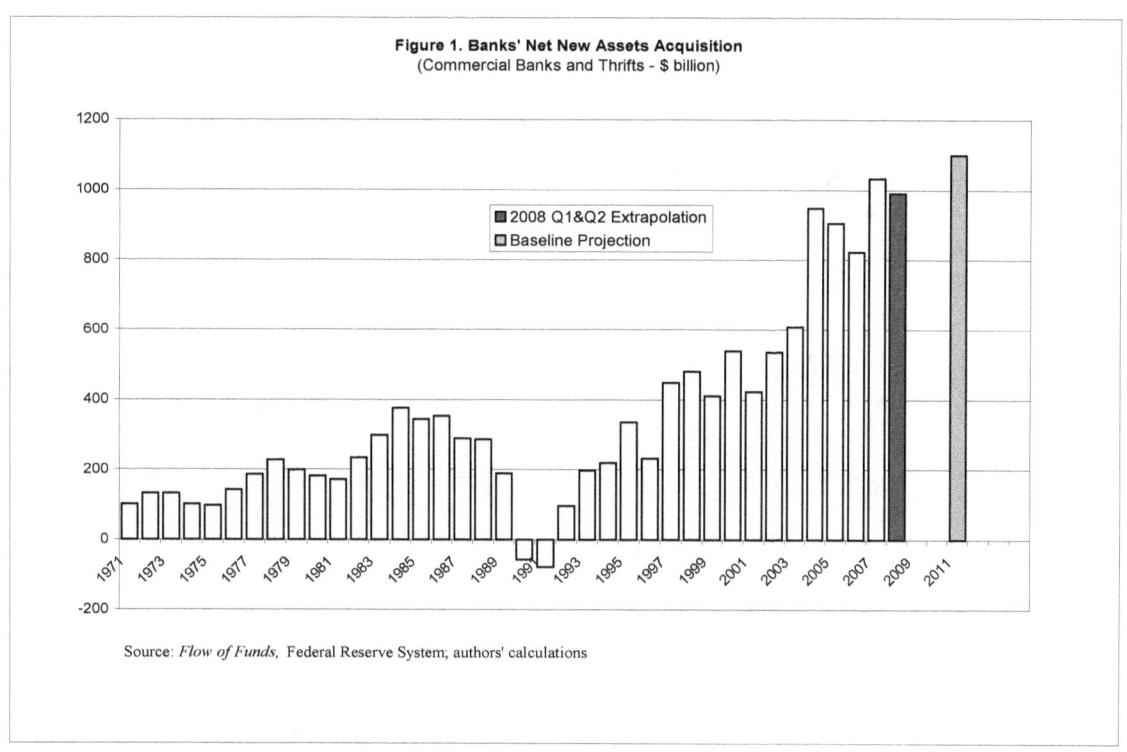

Figure 1. Banks' Net New Assets Acquisition
(Commercial Banks and Thrifts - $ billion)

Source: *Flow of Funds*, Federal Reserve System; authors' calculations

Table 3 contains the last set of preliminary information necessary for our overall credit

extension analysis. The table shows the long-run pattern of credit extension by banks to the

household and business sectors, expressed as a share of bank balance sheet growth. We define

---

remains constant at its first-half 2008 level of 0.073 (compared to its average 0.079 level for the 1970-2007 period), an assumption we posit in the absence of any compelling reason to expect this ratio to change. Doing so means that the annual bank net new asset aquisition growth pace stays roughly in line with its historically average pace over the last four decades. More importantly, the assumption is consistent with companion analysis we have done suggesting that the resultant 2011 target of $1.1 trillion in bank net new asset aquisition is achievable from a funding perspective, but that growth significantly stronger than this would likely be difficult to achieve. Note that to the extent our assumption about the 2011 level of bank net new asset aquisition is considered optimistic, the implications we describe subsequently in the paper for stresses/credit extension challenges faced by nonbank credit providers would become even stronger.

[13] We base our analysis on a pre–FAS 140 world. The FAS 140 change requires banks to move some off-balance-sheet activities, notably credit card trusts, onto balance sheet. The result of this change will be to increase the reported size of banks' balance sheets with the resultant increase in bank credit extension dedicated to financing what were previously off-balance-sheet activities. As such, it would be inappropriate to assume FAS 140–induced balance sheet growth will provide funds available to finance credit extension for purposes other than the previous off-balance-sheet activities. In order to carry out our analysis based on past bank credit extension trends by credit category we, therefore, need to consider the size of banks' balance sheets excluding FAS 140–induced balance sheet expansion. See LaMonte (2009) page 4, and FitchRatings (2009) for explanations of FAS 140 accounting changes and their possible impact on bank balance sheets.

"credit extension" here to include not only new loans held on-balance sheet, but also banks' net new purchases of GSE MBS and banks' net new purchases of corporate bonds.[14] Table 3 shows

							Total Credit Extension (Total Lending + Purchases of GSE Securities + Corporate Bonds)
				Table 3. Bank Credit Extension Patterns: Long-Run Averages for Bank Home Mortgage, Consumer, and Business Lending, and Purchases of Securities (Credit Extension as Percent of Net New Asset Acquisition by Commercial Banks and Thrifts)			
Time Period	Home Mortgage Loans	Consumer Loans	Business Non-Mortgage Loans	Business Mortgage Loans	Bank Purchases of GSE Securities	Bank Purchases of Corporate Bonds[a]	Total Credit Extension (Total Lending + Purchases of GSE Securities + Corporate Bonds)
1971-2000	20.8	9.4	16.7	7.3	8.4	4.1	66.7
1983-2000	19.1	10.6	17.6	7.4	9.0	5.7	69.4
1992-2000	21.3[b]	7.5	15.9	1.9	15.9	5.9	68.4
Parameters used in Baseline Projections	20.0	8.0	17.0	7.0	12.0	5.0	69.0

[a]Includes purchases of foreign and financial sector bonds.
[b]Average 1993-2000 due to anomalies in the home mortgage loan data.
n.a. indicates not applicable.
Sources: *Flow of Funds*, Federal Reserve System; Haver Analytics.

that "total credit extension" to households and businesses amounted to about 70 percent of the long-run (pre-housing market bubble) net new acquisition of assets by banks. Furthermore, the share of net home mortgage lending was relatively stable at about 20 percent of bank balance sheet growth before the housing market bubble emerged. The choice of long-run time period matters somewhat more for some of the other categories of lending but, prior to the housing market bubble, there were no sea changes in the proportion of the balance sheet claimed by the various main credit access sectors. Consequently, we deem it reasonable to expect banks to

---

[14] Note that banks purchase other securities as part of their net new acquisition of assets, such as asset-backed securities based on credit card receivables, but these are not included in our broad analysis because for the industry such purchases are of a much smaller magnitude than the major credit extension elements on which our analysis concentrates. In the *Flow of Funds*, GSEs include Fannie Mae, Freddie Mac, the Federal Home Loan Banks ("FHLBs"), the Government National Mortgage Association ("GNMA" or "Ginnie Mae"), and the Farmers Home Administration ("Farmer Mac").

devote the traditional share of their balance sheets to the various credit sectors going forward based on the relative stability of these shares in the past and the view that the banks chose these shares to obtain their desired asset diversification. With this information in mind, the analysis turns to a consideration of how credit could be extended in 2011, and indeed whether there are grounds for concern about sufficient credit extension by major credit suppliers at normal credit cost.

III. How Might U.S. Home Mortgages Be Financed in 2011?

Net new home mortgage borrowing traditionally has accounted for more than one-third of total annual new borrowing in the U.S. economy. Banks and the GSEs have been the major providers of mortgage credit, and questions about reestablishing long-run stability to the home mortgage market center on these two sectors. In addition, because "private label" securitizers of pools of home mortgages contributed importantly to credit availability even before the post-2000 bubble, we consider the future role of this sector. As outlined in Table 2, in order for home mortgage borrowing to be macroeconomically consistent with the projected $16 trillion GDP in 2011 (representing a moderate recovery level of economic activity), banks, GSEs, and private label MBS issuers would likely have to provide a combined $550 billion in net new mortgage credit.

III.A. Baseline for Financing Home Mortgage Needs in 2011

Banks' home mortgage lending has traditionally accounted for about 20 percent of their net acquisition of financial assets annually, as Table 3 illustrated. Under reasonable assumptions, Figure 1 posited a baseline projection of $1,100 billion in total net acquisition of financial assets for banks. Combining these two patterns yields our baseline of home mortgage lending by banks of $220 billion in 2011, as shown on the "baseline scenario" line of Table 4. (Other scenarios covered in Table 4 are discussed in detail in section III.B.) That would leave $330 billion of new mortgage credit to be provided by some combination of GSE and private label MBS activity.[15]

Table 5 presents key aspects of both banks' and GSEs' traditional roles in providing home mortgage market credit. In particular, over the past two long-run time periods of 1983-2000 and 1992-2000, GSEs provided well over half — 57 percent — of net new home mortgage lending. Were GSEs to finance 55 percent of home mortgage market financing in 2011 — that is, in the same range as their long-run proportion — they would supply $300 billion in net new mortgage credit (Table 4, baseline scenario).[16] In that case, private label MBS issuers would have to supply an additional $30 billion in net new mortgage credit for the combined efforts of banks, GSEs, and private label MBS issuers to reach the $550 billion level. Such a contribution by private label issuers seems credible, as discussed below.

For the baseline scenario to hold, the GSEs would have to finance $300 billion in new mortgage originations by selling approximately this amount of new MBS. Reaching this sales level would not require an unusual pattern of behavior by investors in GSE MBS, and therefore could reasonably be expected to occur without a sharp change in the interest rate on these securities. We expect "traditional investors," following past purchase patterns, to purchase around $100 billion of GSE securities. The four sets of traditional investors in GSE securities

---

[15] Most FHA/VA guaranteed mortgages end up packaged in GNMA-issued MBS.

[16] The $300 billion figure is 55 percent of the total required $550 billion volume of net new mortgage lending consistent with the $16 trillion projected GDP in 2011, as outlined in Table 2.

Table 4. Potential Scenarios for Financing $550 Billion of Home Mortgages in 2011
($ billion, except as noted)

Scenario	Role of GSEs: Net New Agency MBS					Role of Banks		Role of Private Label	Stress Points: Areas where scenario likely requires unrealistically high activity
	GSE Share of Mortgage Market	Total GSE Securiti-zations	Sold to Traditional Investors	Retained by GSEs	Remainder Sold to Banks	Bank Net New Mortgage Loans	Implied Growth in Bank Assets	Total Private Label MBS	
Baseline Scenario: Traditional Financing Patterns	55%	300	100	70	130	220	1100	30	*None*
Scenario 2: Greatly Decreased Role for GSEs (primarily via drop in MBS sales to banks)									
2a: Private label MBS with traditional share, banks pick up slack	25%	150	50	35	65	370	1850	30	Total Bank Assets
2b. Banks with traditional share, private label MBS pick up the slack	25%	150	50	35	65	220	1100	180	Private Label MBS
2c. Both banks and private label MBS pick up the slack	25%	150	50	35	65	295	1475	105	Private Label MBS & Total Bank Assets
Scenario 3: Traditional Share for GSEs, Banks and Private Label MBS Change									
3a: Banks' share declines, slack picked up by private label MBS	55%	300	100	70	130	150	750	100	Private Label MBS
3b. Private Labels do not re-emerge, banks pick up the slack	55%	300	100	70	130	250	1250	0	Total Bank Assets

Key: DARK-shaded cell indicates stress point; LIGHT-shaded cell indicates dollar amount of activity as a key part of baseline scenario.

Table 5. Traditional Home Mortgages Financial Patterns

Time Period	Importance of Home Mortgages:	Role of GSEs:	Role of Banks (Commercial Banks and Thrifts)	
	Net New Home Mortgage Lending as % of Nominal GDP	GSE Financing as % of Net New Home Mortgage Lending	Bank Home Mortgage Lending as % of Banks' Net Financial Asset Acquisition	Bank Purchases of GSE Securities as % of Banks' Net Financial Asset Acquisition
1971-2000	3.4	44.0	20.8	8.4
1983-2000	3.6	57.0	19.1	9.0
1992-2000	3.2[a]	57.0	21.3[a]	15.9

[a] In this cell average is for 1993-2000, because mortgage lending declined in 1992 but banks registered a small increase in the net acquisition of assets that year, resulting in a ratio of dubious meaning.
Sources: *Flow of Funds*, Federal Reserve System; Haver Analytics.

include households and other private entities, foreign investors, life insurance companies, and state and local government pension funds. We have taken a two-step approach to projecting plausible GSE MBS purchase levels for each of these sets. First, we projected investment in all financial assets by each of the four "traditional investor" sets, as shown in row 1 of Table 6. We based these projections on investment flows shown in Figure 2. Life insurance companies' and state and local pension funds' investment levels have been fairly stable over the past decade or more, as can be seen in Figure2, and we assume these levels will continue; we include in the far two right-hand columns in row 1 of Table 6 these typical investment levels (i.e., $250 billion and $25 billion, respectively).[17] Recent investment patterns for "household and other entities" and

---

[17] Rounded to the nearest $5 billion.

	Households and Other Entities	Foreign Investors (U.S. Investment)	Life Insurance Companies	State and Local Pensions
Table 6. GSE Securities Investors: Traditional and 2011 Potential Roles in GSE Securities Purchases				
1. Projected 2011 Total Net Acquisition of Financial Assets	$500 billion	$900 billion	$250 billion	$25 billion
2. 1971-2000 Long-Run Average GSE Securities Purchases as *Percent* of Total Net Acquisition of Financial Assets	5.0	5.0	9.0	13.0
3. *Approximate* Resultant Projection of Purchases of GSE securities[a]	$25 billion	$45 billion	$25 billion	$5 billion
[a] Rounded to nearest $5 billion				

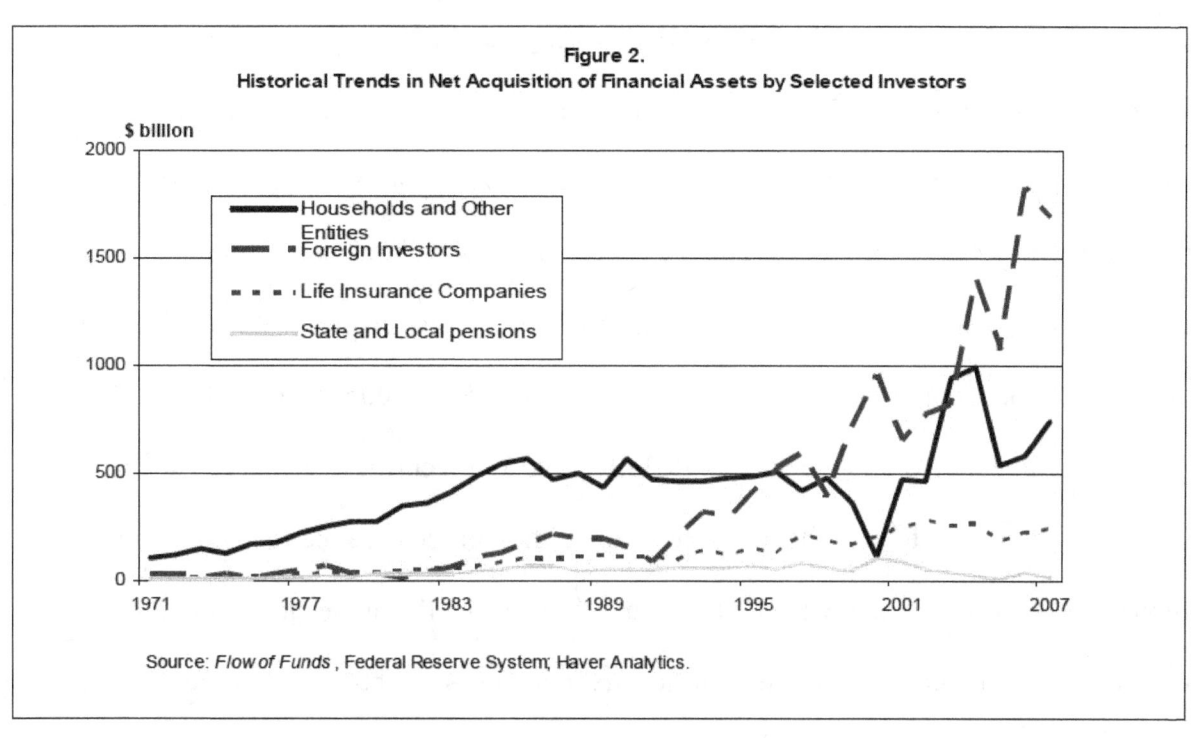

Figure 2.
Historical Trends in Net Acquisition of Financial Assets by Selected Investors

Source: *Flow of Funds*, Federal Reserve System; Haver Analytics.

"foreign investors" have been more erratic, as Figure 2 illustrates.[18] In the absence of definitive modeling to guide our extrapolation of these groups' investment plans, we make a conservative assumption that their investment levels will revert to late 1990–early 2000 amounts ($500 billion and $900 billion for households and other entities and foreign investors, respectively). This conservative assumption is made to bring these investment levels back to pre-bubble ranges as a potential response to the financial crisis. (Given growth in the U.S. and foreign economies during the current decade, it appears likely that these investment levels could well be higher, giving more scope for the GSEs to find ready demand for their MBS.) We next considered the typical share of its total investment each group devotes to buying GSE MBS, shown in the second row of Table 6. Applying this typical share to the projected level of total investment in row 1 yielded the projected levels of demand for GSE MBS by each group in 2011, shown in row 3 of Table 6, as follows: households and other entities: $25 billion; foreign investors: $45 billion; life insurance companies: $25 billion; and state and local (government) pension plans: $5 billion. Altogether, the four investor groups could be expected, under reasonable assumptions, to purchase $100 billion of the $300 billion worth of GSE securities shown in the baseline scenario of Table 4 without requiring a sharp rise in interest payments to induce them to do so.

If traditional investors purchase $100 billion of GSE securities, then banks and the GSEs themselves would have to hold the remaining $200 billion of the baseline issuance of $300 billion GSE MBS. Traditionally the GSEs have retained a significant portion of their net issuance of MBS. Figure 3 shows the historical trend in GSEs' retention of their newly issued MBS. Under the assumption that by 2011 the GSEs will have scaled back considerably from their peak levels of retention, the baseline scenario in Table 4 shows GSE retention of new MBS

---

[18] In the *Flow of Funds* the category "households and other private entities" is a (large) residual group; it includes hedge funds.

in 2011 at $70 billion. The remaining purchases by banks of GSE MBS issued in 2011 would, consequently, have to be $130 billion to yield total GSE MBS sales amounting to $300 billion. Such a level of GSE securities purchases by banks would be consistent with the long-run pattern of bank purchases of GSE securities shown in Table 5. In particular, were banks to purchase $130 billion in GSE securities in 2011, out of their baseline $1,100 billion in total net new asset aquisition, that would amount to 12 percent of total net new bank assets, a proportion clearly in line with the 8.4 percent to 15.9 percent range listed in the far right-hand column of Table 5 as part of banks' long-run pattern of home mortgage financing.

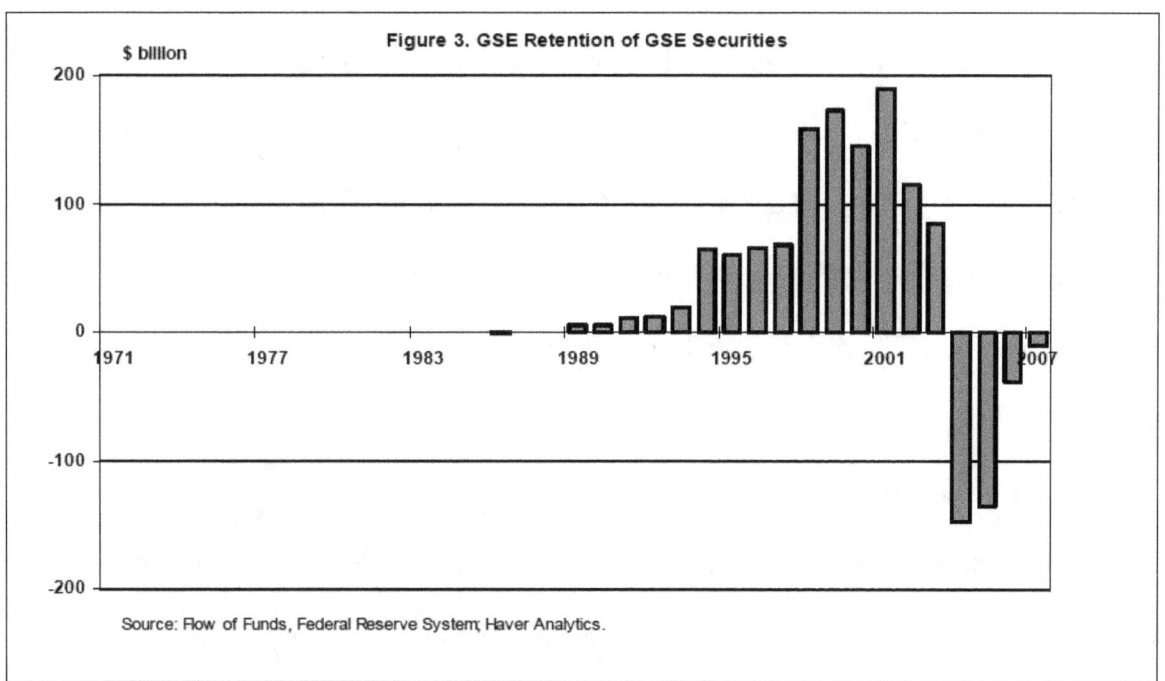

The third major player in home mortgage provision, private label MBS issuers, could reasonably be expected to finance the $30 billion in net new home mortgages shown in the first line of Table 4. In particular, the GSEs do not securitize jumbo mortgage loans (i.e., those for amounts above $625,000); in the absence of any significant reemergence by 2011 of the

17

subprime mortgage market, it is conceivable that private label MBS issuers could manage to sell $30 billion of securitized pools of high-quality jumbo mortgages. We base this assumption on the observation that, even as the mortgage market rapidly soured in 2008, new issuance of private label mortgage securities totaled $38 billion over the first eight months of 2008. Under these circumstances, $30 billion in jumbo-mortgage-based private label MBS seems conservative.

III.B. Possible Alternative Home Mortgage Financing Scenarios

Section III.A described a baseline scenario reflecting traditional financing patterns, as summarized in the top row of Table 4. Table 4 also conveys the consequences for the other two sectors of a deviation from traditional financing patterns by any one of the three major mortgage credit providers. That is, it considers the overall feasibility of situations in which one of the three main home mortgage credit providers supplies less than the baseline scenario. Could the other two sectors be expected to pick up the slack without a substantial spike in mortgage interest rates?

Scenario variations 2a, 2b, and 2c in Table 4 consider the possibility that the GSEs substantially decrease their role in the provision of home mortgage credit.[19] Each of the variations of Scenario 2 illustrated in Table 4 begins with the assumption that GSEs' home mortgage market role is cut from $300 billion (i.e., 55 percent) to $150 billion of net new home mortgage credit in 2011. That change would result in total GSE securitizations of $150 billion.[20]

---

[19] There is an active debate on the future of the GSEs, and one line of reasoning calls for a greatly reduced role for them as a prelude to their restructuring and subsequent sale to the private sector. The Department of the Treasury's white paper *Financial Regulatory Reform: A New Foundation* (June 2009) outlines five major options "for the reform of the GSEs." See pp. 41 and 42 in particular.

[20] Under the Scenario 2 variations of halving of GSE's MBS issuance, we assume for simplicity that investors (i.e., traditional investors, banks, and the GSEs themselves) halve their investment in GSE MBS issuance, as shown in

How could the $150 billion reduction in the GSEs' contribution to total new mortgage credit provision be addressed?

The first issue to be addressed is whether the money presumed in the baseline to be invested in GSE securities would find its way to finance home mortgages through another channel without a substantial adjustment in interest rates. This possibility appears very unlikely. The purchasers of GSE securities would likely channel their investments into other U.S. and foreign government securities since these investors are typically in the market for high credit quality and very liquid securities, making private label MBS an unlikely substitute. Moreover, the securities are often used for trading, collateral, and securities-lending purposes, making bank accounts an unlikely substitute. Given these considerations, a pullback of GSE mortgage lending would likely have to be offset by an increase in bank lending or private label MBS without funding inflow from the erstwhile GSE MBS investors.

Scenario 2a looks at the possibility of banks picking up all of the slack. Were banks to add $150 billion to their "baseline" net new mortgage lending, they would be financing $370 billion of new home mortgage loans in total. For that to happen, banks would either have to sharply increase the size of their balance sheets if they wanted to keep home mortgage lending to only its normal 20 percent share of their net new asset aquisition or, if banks chose to increase mortgages as a share of their asset aquisition while keeping their balance sheet growth in check, they would have to sharply cut back the share of credit extension to other areas. In the former case, were home mortgages to remain at the long-run 20 percent of banks' balance sheet growth, banks would have to expand their overall net asset acquisition to $1,850 billion; that, in turn, means that banks' assets would have to grow almost eight times faster than GDP, a highly

---

Table 4, but that particular pattern of the distribution of the lower issuance of GSE MBS among the three investors is not necessary for our analysis to carry forward.

19

unrealistic outcome. In the latter case, where banks shift lending to home mortgages at the expense of lending to other sectors while bank balance sheets grow by only $1,100 billion, banks would have to ramp up their home mortgage lending by 68 percent over their baseline level that was consistent with $1,100 billion of net new asset aquisition. In the wake of the recent mortgage crisis it is hardly plausible that banks would expand their home mortgage lending to such a degree without an extremely sharp rise in mortgage interest rates. Consequently, under either alternative, banks do not appear positioned to pick up the slack from a significant pullback of the GSEs in a scenario where mortgage financing costs remain moderate.

Suppose then that banks maintain their traditional share of net asset aquisition devoted to home mortgages while experiencing a growth in total net asset acquisition of $1,100 billion, and therefore provide only $220 billion in net new home mortgage loans. Might private label mortgage securitizations pick up the GSEs' shortfall? Scenario 2b suggests that this is unlikely, for it would mean a six-fold increase of private label MBS issuance over its baseline level, to $180 billion from $30 billion. For private label issuers heretofore focusing on securitizing pools of subprime and nontraditional mortgages, the necessity of radically changing their business model and, simultaneously, securing sufficient investor confidence is likely to present significant obstacles over a relatively short period. Under these circumstances, there is little reason to suppose that private MBS issuers would be able to pick up much of the slack were GSE issuance to slide substantially.

What about a middle ground then, where a reduced GSE role in the mortgage market is made up in part by greater bank lending and in part by private label MBS issuance? Scenario 2c considers this possibility, assigning to banks one-half of the GSE shortfall ($75 billion additional mortgage lending) and half to private label securitizers. Under these circumstances, were banks to maintain their long-run 20 percent of net new asset acquisition for home mortgages, overall growth of bank asset acquisitions would need to be $1,450 billion. That level would be above what banks could be expected to undertake in the midst of a moderate recovery of economic activity in 2011. Alternatively, if banks did add $75 billion in additional home mortgages while their balance sheets grew by only $1,100 billion, they would end up increasing their mortgage lending by 34 percent above the level consistent with a traditional portfolio share for that type of mortgage lending of about 20 percent of balance sheet growth. In light of the so-far slow and uncertain recovery of the mortgage market, this outcome appears unlikely unless mortgage rates were to dramatically rise. Furthermore, the addition of $75 billion to the mortgage credit provision total for private label MBS issuers looks unrealistically high for the reasons discussed in the preceding paragraph.

Finally, suppose the GSEs maintain their 55 percent long-run mortgage credit provision share but that banks and private label issuers play a reduced role in the mortgage market: could the slack be taken up elsewhere? Scenario variations 3a and 3b in Table 4 investigate the two major possibilities. First, suppose, with GSEs retaining their long-run trend share of mortgage credit provision, banks find their role reduced somewhat. Scenario 3a looks at the case where banks' net new acquisition of mortgage loans declines to $150 billion from its baseline $220 billion. It seems certain that banks could reach a level of total net new asset aquisition of $750 billion implied under this circumstance, with home mortgages remaining 20 percent of bank balance sheet growth. However, private label MBS issuers would have to pick up the $70 billion slack caused by banks' actions, resulting in private label issuers having to provide $100 billion in mortgage credit. The only way that could happen is if, contrary to our underlying framework,

21

borrowers were willing to pay radically higher mortgage rates in order to increase investor demand for these securities.[21]

Scenario variation 3b looks at the situation in which private label MBS are not issued, while GSEs continue to supply 55 percent of mortgage demand. Would banks make up for the MBS shortfall? If banks kept mortgages at their long-run average (20 percent of banks' net new asset acquisition), the answer is "probably not," because that would imply a substantially higher-than-baseline $1,250 billion in bank balance sheet growth in 2011. If banks picked up the slack by shifting away from business and other consumer lending instead of balance sheet expansion, the result would be that banks increase home mortgage credit by 14 percent above the level representing 20 percent of bank balance sheet growth. This also does not look like a probable outcome.

In summary, under realistic assumptions it appears that mortgage market financing in line with a moderate recovery level of GDP can emerge in the credit markets. However, that outcome depends crucially on GSE mortgage securitizations at long-run trend levels of about 55 percent of net new home mortgage financing. Banks could be expected to provide mortgage financing consistent with their long-run role, including indirectly as substantial purchasers of GSE mortgage-backed securities. Furthermore, a modest recovery of private label mortgage securitizations, centering perhaps on high-quality jumbo mortgages (rather than, as in the recent past, on subprime loans) is easily conceivable. Under these circumstances, GSEs would be able to sell the requisite level of net new securitizations not only to banks, but to traditional investors as well. If, however, GSEs were to decrease their net new issuance of MBS substantially below their long-run level, either for economic reasons or in response to public policy pressures aimed at intentionally reducing their role in the mortgage market, it appears unlikely that either banks

---

[21] Calculation of such significant interest rate/securities price adjustments is beyond the scope of this paper.

or the private label market would pick up the slack — unless, of course, the returns that banks and/or private label investors receive were to rise substantially.

IV. How Might U.S. Consumer Borrowing Be Financed in 2011?

Net new consumer borrowing traditionally has accounted for a bit less than 10 percent of total annual new borrowing in the U.S. economy. The major providers of consumer credit are banks, issuers of securities backed by pools of nonmortgage consumer loans ("ABS issuers"), and finance companies and other nonbanks (see Table 7). Table 7 shows that finance companies and other nonbank providers of consumer credit have maintained a relatively constant one-third share of consumer credit provision.[22] In contrast, the relative importance of banks on the one hand and ABS issuers on the other has shifted greatly.[23] In particular, the more recent the long-run period considered, the larger the role of ABS issuers in the provision of consumer credit relative to banks. Looking at the 1992-2000 period, ABS issuers accounted for more than twice the proportion of new consumer lending as did banks, and almost half (46.1 percent) of total new consumer credit extension. It is clear that even before the post-2000 period of aggressive leveraging-up, ABS issuers had become the dominant funding source for consumer borrowing. As a consequence, any analysis of the future pattern of consumer credit provision must make the role of ABS issuers a central focus.

---

[22] "Other nonbank providers" of consumer credit include nonfinancial corporate business, nonfarm noncorporate business, the GSEs, credit unions, and the federal government.

[23] Several large banks play a important role in the issuance of credit card ABS, making the bank-structured finance relationship a complicated one, as Box 2 at the end of this paper explains.

Table 7. Long-Run Patterns of Funding for Net New Consumer Borrowing: Banks and Other Sources (Percent of Net New Consumer Credit Extension)				
Long-Run Time Periods	ABS Issuers	Banks (Commercial Banks and Thrifts)	Finance Cos.	Other Nonbank Providers
1971-2000	31.5	34.5	13.0	20.9
1983-2000	37.8	30.3	10.8	21.1
1992-2000	46.1	22.3	10.9	20.8

Sources: *Flow of Funds*, Federal Reserve System; Haver Analytics.

The sharp contraction in the market for structured finance products is a hallmark of the ongoing financial system crisis.[24] A major dimension of this contraction was the collapse of the consumer credit ABS market, as Box 1 at the end of this paper illustrates. With this recent cratering of the role of ABS issuers in mind, we turn to a consideration of the possible nature of consumer credit provision in 2011.

We first project the level of likely consumer credit demand in 2011. Given that before the recent credit bubble consumer credit demand traditionally averaged about 1.2 percent of nominal GDP (as shown on Table 1), we can project a 2011 "normal" level of consumer credit demand of $190 billion (Table 2), consistent with our projection of $16 trillion nominal GDP that year.[25] How can this level of demand be met?

---

[24] Nolle (2009) emphasizes the role of structured finance in the current financial crisis as compared to previous financial downturns. Barth et al. (2009) offers a detailed explanation of the connections between the mortgage market meltdown and the contraction in the consumer ABS market.

[25] Our use of long-run averages from pre-bubble time periods avoids a reliance on recent levels of activity, which are likely to have been distorted by the factors that led to asset price bubbles in the first place. As the current financial turmoil continues, a consensus is emerging that consumers' new propensity to save is not a short-run change in behavior, but rather is likely to signal a longer-lived shift. For example, after personal-saving-to-disposable-personal income (DPI) ratios of 2 percent or lower during the bubble years, in Q1 2009 the saving-to-DPI ratio rose to 4.3

Suppose, first, that the consumer-loan-backed securitization market remains moribund through 2011: how different would banks' and other consumer credit providers' behavior have to be to fill the credit hole left by that development, consistent with moderate economic growth? Scenario 1 in Table 8 considers two main variations under the presumption that consumer ABS issuance does not recover in the near future. Variation 1a begins by considering the consequences of banks providing net new consumer loans consistent with $1,100 billion in total net new bank asset aquisition, established in the previous section as a reasonable "baseline" overall level. From Table 3, and in a manner parallel to the calculations in the previous section on home mortgage credit, we use an approximation of the long-run average pattern of consumer lending by banks. In particular, assuming banks were to continue to devote approximately 8 percent of their net new asset acquisition to consumer loans, baseline total asset acquisition of $1,100 billion for banks means that they would provide about $90 billion in new consumer loans in 2011. The "Role of Banks" columns under Scenario 1a in Table 8 show this.

If ABS issuers fail to support new consumer borrowing, and banks lend at their baseline level, would finance companies and other nonbanks be able to pick up the slack? Scenario 1a suggests they would find that task very challenging. Out of the total $190 billion in net new consumer borrowing that is consistent with nominal GDP of $16 trillion, were banks to provide the $90 billion consistent with their baseline net asset acquisition level, finance companies and other nonbanks would have to provide the remaining $100 billion. Scenario 1a in Table 8 assigns $35 billion of the $100 billion shortfall in consumer credit provision to finance companies and

---

percent. In effect, our use of longer-run trends to establish baseline scenarios incorporates this shift: the personal-saving-to-DPI ratio during the 1992-2000 period averaged 4.4 percent. In a similar vein, some observers have noted that because of large declines in home prices, household wealth has dropped substantially, a development that could affect consumer spending and therefore consumers' demand for credit. As in the case of household savings rates, the long-run, pre-bubble trend periods we use to establish baseline scenarios also had similar household-wealth-to-DPI ratios as those beginning to emerge after the bubble years. For example, the ratio of household-net-worth to DPI dropped from 6.3 in 2006 and 2007 at the height of the bubble to 5.4 in 2008, in line with the 1992-2000 annual average ratio of household-net-worth to DPI.

Table 8. Potential Scenarios for Financing $190 Billion of Consumer Borrowing in 2011
($ billion, except as noted)

Scenario	Role of ABS Issuers		Role of Banks		Role of Finance Companies		Role of Nonbank Providers		Stress Points Areas Where Scenario Likely Requires Unrealistically High Activity
	ABS Issuance Share of Consumer Credit Provision	Total ABS Issuance	Bank Net New Consumer Lending	Implied Growth in Bank Assets	Finance Co. Share of Consumer Credit Provision	Finance Companies Net New Consumer Lending	Nonbank Share of Consumer Credit Provision	Total Nonbank Provision of Consumer Credit	
Scenario 1: ABS Issuance Does Not Reemerge									
1a. Banks provide sustainable level of consumer credit, nonbank providers pick up the slack.	0%	0	90	1100	19%	35	33%	65	Growth in total finance company assets and in other nonbank assets
1b. Nonbank providers of consumer credit resume long-run pattern of lending, banks pick up the slack.	0%	0	130	1600	12%	20	21%	40	Growth in total bank assets
Scenario 2: Reemergence of ABS Issuance									
Minimum necessary ABS Issuance re-emergence consistent with sustainable level of consumer credit provided by banks, and finance companies and other nonbank providers resume long-run patterns of consumer lending.	21%	40	90	1100	12%	20	21%	40	None; however, reemergence of ABS market is crucial

Key: DARK-shaded cell indicates stress point; LIGHT-shaded cell indicates dollar amount of activity as a likely part of an overall feasible scenario.

26

the remaining $65 billion to other nonbanks, broadly in line with historical proportions as shown in Table 7.

Those amounts both appear unrealistically high. In particular, they would mean that finance companies would have to provide 19 percent of total new consumer lending, a share almost double their long-run share; and $65 billion worth of consumer credit provision by other nonbanks would give them a 35 percent share of total consumer credit provision, a proportion two-thirds again as high as their long-run levels. It is difficult to imagine that either set of players' capital base or underwriting standards would stretch so far, over such a short period of time.

Scenario 1b considers the opposite alternative — that is, a failure of the revival of the consumer ABS market resulting in banks picking up all the slack, while finance companies and other nonbanks contribute at their long-run average proportions of 12 percent and 21 percent, respectively, of the total necessary $190 billion new consumer credit. In this case, as the "Role of Banks" columns under Scenario 1b show, banks would have to provide the difference between the $60 billion net new consumer credit provided by finance companies ($20 billion) and other nonbanks ($40 billion), and the necessary $190 billion. Addressing the entire $130 billion shortfall looks like an unrealistic stretch for banks. That is because, if banks do not devote a disproportionately greater share than the long-run average 8 percent of their net asset acquisition to consumer loans, the $130 billion level of new consumer lending implies total bank net asset aquisition in 2011 of over $1,600 billion. Such a level is more than 45 percent above the baseline $1,100 billion. Alternatively, if banks supply the entire $130 billion in consumer finance while keeping their balance sheet growth at only $1,100 billion, they would be raising their amount of consumer financing by 44 percent (i.e., an additional $40 billion) above the baseline level consistent with its long-run share of bank balance sheet growth ($90 billion). Given the recent history of consumer defaults and incipient changes in credit card regulations, such an increase seems unlikely for banks or, for that matter, any other suppliers of consumer credit without an extremely sharp rise in consumer credit cost.

Scenarios 1a and 1b show that, in the absence of large adjustments in the price of consumer credit, it is very unlikely that banks, finance companies, and other nonbank consumer credit providers would fill the entire void in the consumer credit market caused by the total absence of ABS issuers. Scenario 2 in the bottom portion of Table 8 asks what the level of participation by ABS issuers would have to be if the other providers of consumer credit reached their long-run average share of credit provision in 2011. We label that level the "minimum" level of participation by ABS issuers on the idea that, because there are no compelling reasons to expect either banks, finance companies, or other nonbank participants to contribute much above their long-run shares in the near future, ABS issuers would have to re-emerge in at least sufficient force to fill the gap left by a return to no more than long-run average credit provision by the rest of the market.[26]

Scenario 2 in Table 8 puts bank net new consumer credit extension at $90 billion, consistent with $1,100 billion overall net asset acquisition by banks. Finance companies and other nonbanks supply consumer credit in line with their long-run average shares of, respectively, 12 percent and 21 percent of the total demand for net new consumer borrowing. Together, banks, finance companies, and other nonbanks therefore would provide $150 billion in

---

[26] Indeed, for both finance companies and other nonbank providers we believe the expectation of return to long-run levels might be somewhat optimistic. Finance companies tend to have a greater focus on less credit-worthy customers than do banks, and that market looks set to languish in the near term; and, as pointed out in footnote 22, the category of "other nonbank providers" is in fact made up of several smallish sub-entities, none of which could by itself be expected to greatly boost the group's total participation.

consumer credit, leaving ABS issuers to supply the remaining $40 billion necessary to bring total new consumer credit to the required $190 billion. For ABS issuers, that means they would have to supply 21 percent of total new consumer credit, not quite half of their pre-2001 share.

The likelihood of consumer ABS issuance reemerging from very low levels currently to a level in line with Scenario 2 is more difficult to guess at than was the case in the previous section's discussion of possible responses of investors in GSE MBS. Under these circumstances, initiatives such as the Term Asset-Backed Securities Loan Facility ("TALF") program, designed to reignite investor interest in the ABS market, may help in this regard.

V. How Might U.S. Business Sector Credit Be Financed in 2011?

The business sector needs credit both for current operations and for future growth.[27] Businesses borrow from banks and other lenders, but in contrast to the household sector, larger businesses can also attract financing directly from the capital markets. Bond sales traditionally account for a large share of business financing, while businesses' commercial paper sales account for a more moderate share of total credit extension to the sector. Businesses' mortgage debt is also supported by issuers of commercial mortgage-backed securities (CMBS), securitized pools of commercial mortgages. At around 4 ½ percent of nominal GDP over the long run (see Table 1), net new business borrowing has been approximately equal to net new home mortgage borrowing and net new consumer borrowing combined. A declining but still significant portion of business sector borrowing centers on business mortgage borrowing supplied by banks and other lenders (see Table 1).[28]

---

[27] Unless specifically stated otherwise, in this paper the term "business sector" refers to nonfinancial businesses.

[28] The decline in bank-financed business mortgage borrowing coincides with the recent surge in the issuance of CMBS (illustrated in Figure 7, and discussed below).

Table 3 highlights the importance of business sector credit extension for banks. First, lending to the business sector has accounted for around 17 percent of total bank net financial asset acquisition. Banks' business sector mortgage lending varied more across the long-run time periods shown in Table 3. We assume, however, that the low proportion of business mortgage lending over the 1992-2000 period is a less reliable guide than the two longer time periods, particularly in light of the ongoing shutdown of the CMBS market (see Box 1 at the end of this paper); under these circumstances, we judge that businesses may be more, rather than less, reliant on bank financing for mortgage credit extension, and hence look for guidance to the patterns over the 1971-2000 and 1983-2000 periods, using a ratio of 7 percent of net asset aquisition for banks' business mortgage lending in our baseline projections. Banks also provide indirect support to the financing of business sector credit needs by purchasing corporate bonds, accounting on average for about 5 percent of banks' net financial asset acquisition, as shown in Table 3. Referring back to Table 2, note that business borrowing from all sources has to be at a level of about $720 billion to be consistent with moderate growth in nominal GDP to $16 trillion by 2011. Table 9 lays out scenarios for how that total amount of business credit might be financed, highlighting in particular alternatives where obstacles could arise.

V.A. Baseline for Financing Business Credit Needs in 2011

Scenario 1 shows a feasible combination of credit provision to the business sector by banks, bond sales, commercial paper sales, CMBS issuance, and lending by traditional investors

Table 9. Potential Scenarios for Supplying $720 Billion of Nonfinancial Business Sector Credit in 2011 ($ billion)

Scenario	Bank Net New Non-Mortgage Lending	Role of Banks					Bond Sales				Commercial Paper	CMBS	Other Lenders			Stress Points
		Implied Growth in Bank Assets	Bank Net New Mortgage Lending	Implied Growth in Bank Assets	Bank Purchases of Bonds	Implied Growth in Bank Assets	Total (Including Bonds Purchased by Banks)	Sold to Institutional Investors	Sold to Private Entities	Sold to Foreigners			Total	Traditional Investors	ABS Issuers	Areas where Scenario likely requires unrealistically high activity
1. Baseline: Resumption of Long-Run Trends	185	1100	75	1100	30	1100	315	200	30	55	25	50	70	60	10	None
2. Commercial Paper market does not revive	195	1150	75	1100	30	1100	330	205	35	60	0	50	70	60	10	Banks' balance sheets stretched, but feasible.
3. Large net decline in Commercial Paper market	195	1150	75	1100	30	1100	460	275	35	120	-160	50	100	90	10	Banks' balance sheets, Other Lenders, and Bond sales stretched, but feasible.
4. Bond purchases drop substantially	195	1150	75	1100	25	1000	250	165	25	35	25	50	125	90	35	Banks' balance sheets stretched but feasible. ABS Issuers' lending NOT feasible.
5. Banks' bond purchases make up for declining other bond demand.	185	1100	75	1100	90	3500	315	165	25	35	25	50	70	60	10	Banks' required bond purchases stretch balance sheets to Unfeasible level.
6. Decline by "Other Lenders"	195	1150	75	1100	30	1100	330	210	30	60	25	50	45	40	5	Banks' balance sheets stretched but feasible
7. Large decline in CMBS	185	1100	95	1350	30	1100	315	200	30	55	25	30	70	60	10	Banks' balance sheets stretched to Unfeasible levels

KEY:
BOLD-ITALIC LARGEST FONT cell indicates feasible Baseline.
LIGHT-GRAY cell indicates Stretched but Feasible outcome.
BLACK cell with WHITE numerals indicates Stressed variable.
DARK-GRAY cell indicates Unfeasible outcome.
GRAY cell with WHITE numerals indicates major financing entries.
WHITE cell indicates financing subentry.

Note: Under some scenarios bank balance sheet growth is shown to vary across asset categories. Of course, if the scenario were to occur, bank balance sheet growth could only be one specific amount. The different amounts shown above are meant to highlight where stress could occur because bank asset accumulation in a specific asset category would be substantially out of line with its historical average share. Criteria used to decide which outcomes are stretched but feasible as opposed to infeasible are described in the text.

and ABS issuers. Consider first the role of banks. As established in the previous sections, banks could be expected to generate around $1,100 billion in total net asset acquisition in 2011. As illustrated in Table 3, banks typically have allocated about 17 percent of their net financial asset acquisition to business sector nonmortgage lending, and hence could be expected to extend $185 billion of such lending in 2011. Similarly, as Scenario 1 in Table 9 shows, at about 7 percent of net financial asset acquisition, banks could be counted to make about $75 billion in net new business sector mortgage loans.

A second large element of the baseline top-row Scenario 1 in Table 9 is bond financing for businesses. Key to this element of the scenario is the participation level of traditional bond purchasers. Based on typical bond purchasing patterns we think $315 billion in net new business sector bond sales in 2011 is feasible.[29] Banks typically commit about 5 percent of their net financial asset acquisition to a combination of both U.S. and foreign corporate bond purchases. Probably about half of these purchases are of U.S. nonfinancial corporate bonds.[30] Banks could therefore be expected to devote about 2 ½ percent of their 2011 net asset aquisition to purchases of U.S. corporate bonds. On a basis of total net financial asset aquisition of $1,100 billion, banks would thus buy about $30 billion of the projected $315 billion total net new U.S. corporate bond issuance.

Bond purchases by U.S. institutional investors have followed a fairly stable pattern in the past and, on those trends, institutional investors could be expected to purchase about $200 billion of business sector bond issuance, as shown in row 1 of Table 9. Private U.S. entities, including

---

[29] As explained below, bond sales significantly higher than this level are also credible.

[30] *Flow of Funds* data indicate about half of total U.S. and foreign bond purchases covered in its data, which includes bonds purchased by banks, traditionally consists of U.S. nonfinancial corporate bonds. We assume the composition of bank bond purchases matches this aggregate bond purchase composition.

hedge funds, endowments, and households, have been significant purchasers of corporate bonds as well. A substantial share of hedge funds have closed over the course of the current financial turmoil; this factor suggests that private entities are likely to reduce bond purchases to a level more in line with their 1990s–early 2000s, pre-bubble patterns illustrated in Figure 4. Figure 4

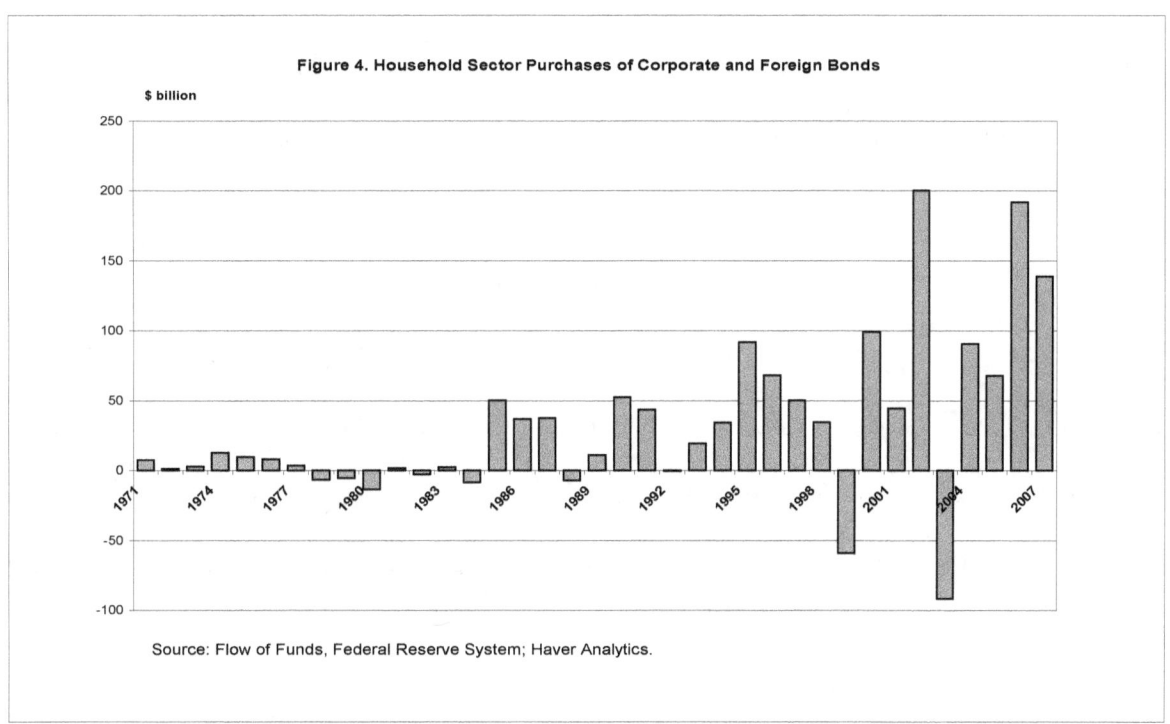

Figure 4. Household Sector Purchases of Corporate and Foreign Bonds

Source: Flow of Funds, Federal Reserve System; Haver Analytics.

shows that purchases of roughly $60 billion in U.S. and foreign bonds would not be inconsistent with recent experience; because U.S. nonfinancial bonds traditionally have accounted for about half of these bonds, we assume that private entities could be expected to purchase approximately $30 billion in bonds.[31]

---

[31] We project household and other private entity purchases of corporate bonds slightly differently than we did their purchases of GSE securities. There appears to be a general uptrend in the share of net new financial asset aquisition they have devoted to corporate bonds, unlike the case with GSE securities.

Foreign purchases of U.S. financial sector assets are significant, including in the U.S. corporate bond market, a point illustrated in Figure 5.[32] In light of the generally more conservative posture by both foreign and domestic investors as well as the increased supply of U.S. government securities on the market, we conclude that foreign purchases of U.S. corporate bonds are likely to retreat. However, we think it is reasonable to assume these purchases at least amount to $55 billion in 2011, as shown in Scenario 1 in Table 9.[33] At that level, foreign purchases would bring total net new purchases of U.S. nonfinancial corporate bonds to the $315 billion target.

The third source of financing considered in Table 9 is commercial paper issuance. Net new issuance of commercial paper has shown a good deal of volatility over the post-2000 bubble period as Figure 6 illustrates. Prior to that, net new nonfinancial business commercial paper borrowing approached $25 billion on a number of occasions. We expect borrowing to reach that level in 2011. Section V.B discusses how a shortfall in that level probably could be addressed by alternative funding.

---

[32] Data is only available for foreign purchases of U.S. nonfinancial sector and financial sector bonds combined. We assume that the share of these purchases devoted to nonfinancial sector bonds mirrors the share of nonfinancial sector bonds in total (combined nonfinancial and financial sector) bond issuance in the United States each year.

[33] This $55 billion projection puts foreign purchases of corporate bonds at 6 percent of total projected foreign investor net new acquisition of U.S.-based assets in 2011 (see row 1 of Table 6 for our total foreign net new asset aquisition projection). Recall that our total foreign net new asset aquisition projection was already subdued in that it assumed foreign demand retreated to its turn of the decade level. The long-run average share of foreign net new acquisition of U.S.-based assets held by U.S. corporate and financial sector bonds combined is 18 percent, suggesting that a 6 percent projected share for corporate bonds alone probably puts foreign corporate bond purchases below their long-run average share. Consequently, a projected $55 billion in corporate bond sales to foreigners is a conservative assumption.

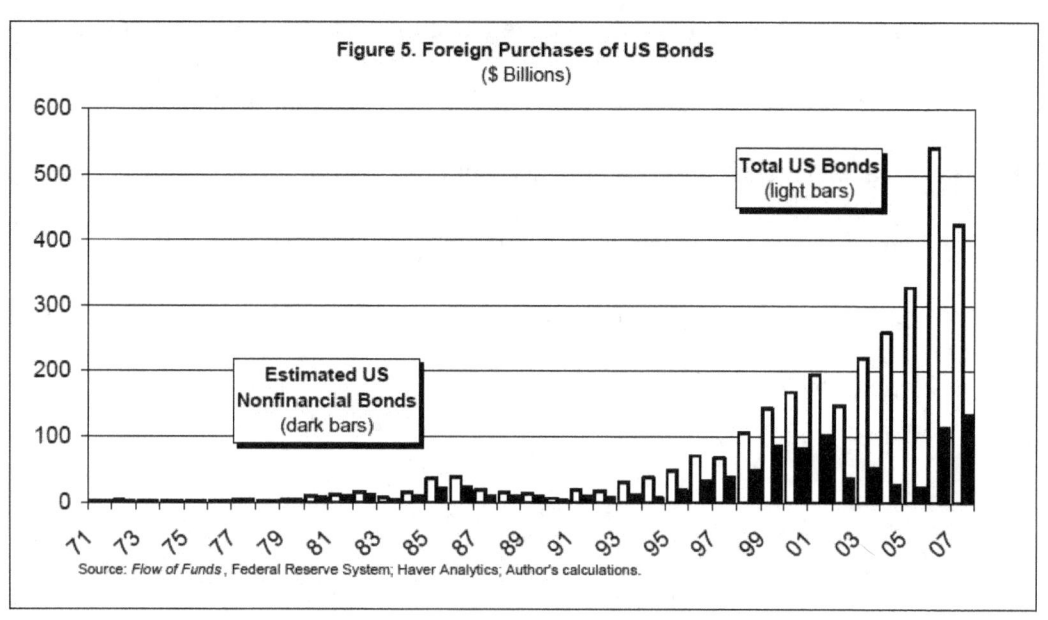

Figure 5. Foreign Purchases of US Bonds
($ Billions)

Source: *Flow of Funds*, Federal Reserve System; Haver Analytics; Author's calculations.

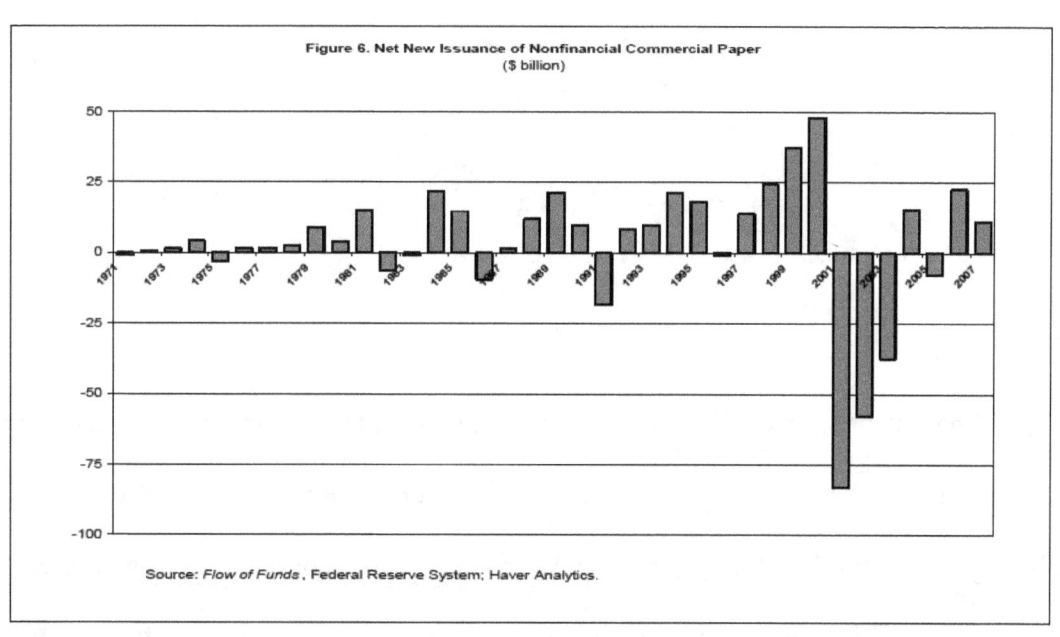

Figure 6. Net New Issuance of Nonfinancial Commercial Paper
($ billion)

Source: *Flow of Funds*, Federal Reserve System; Haver Analytics.

A fourth source of financing for the business sector, and one of great concern recently, is commercial mortgage-backed securities issuance (CMBS). As with other forms of structured finance, CMBS issuance surged in the recent past, but then declined precipitously in 2008. We posit a baseline level of CMBS issuance of $50 billion, representing a considerable pullback from recent levels, as illustrated in Figure 7. Section V.B argues that a sharp shortfall from that level would be difficult to make up elsewhere.

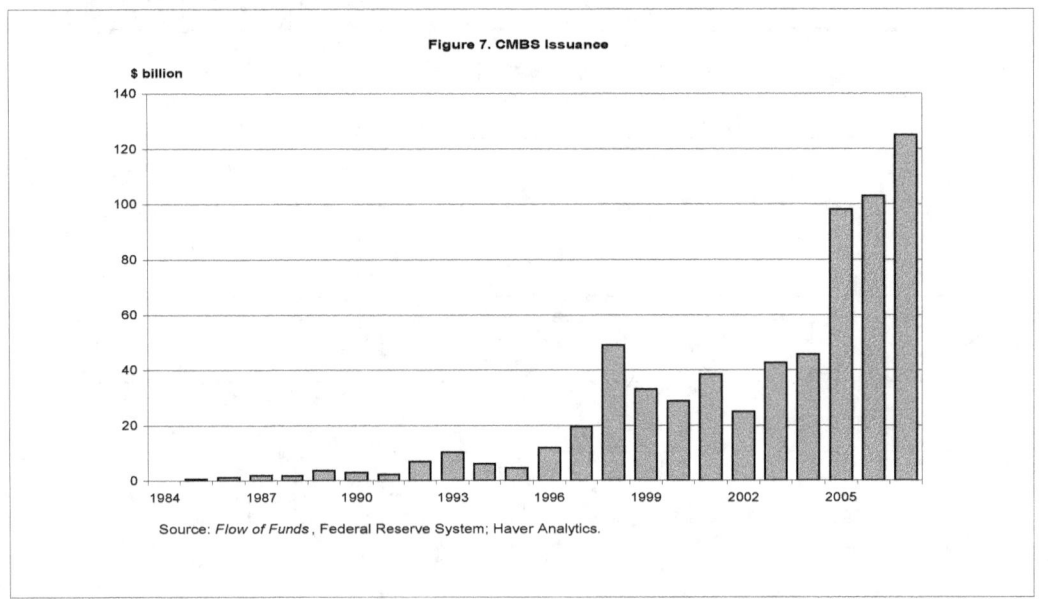

The final major source of business sector financing is lending from nonbank entities, including in particular traditional investors and ABS issuers, as indicated in Table 9. Figures 8 and 9 show the pattern of lending from those two sources to the nonfinancial business sector. We assume that traditional investors, such as life insurance companies and mutual funds, contribute about $60 billion to business financing, and ABS issuance runs at about $10 billion.

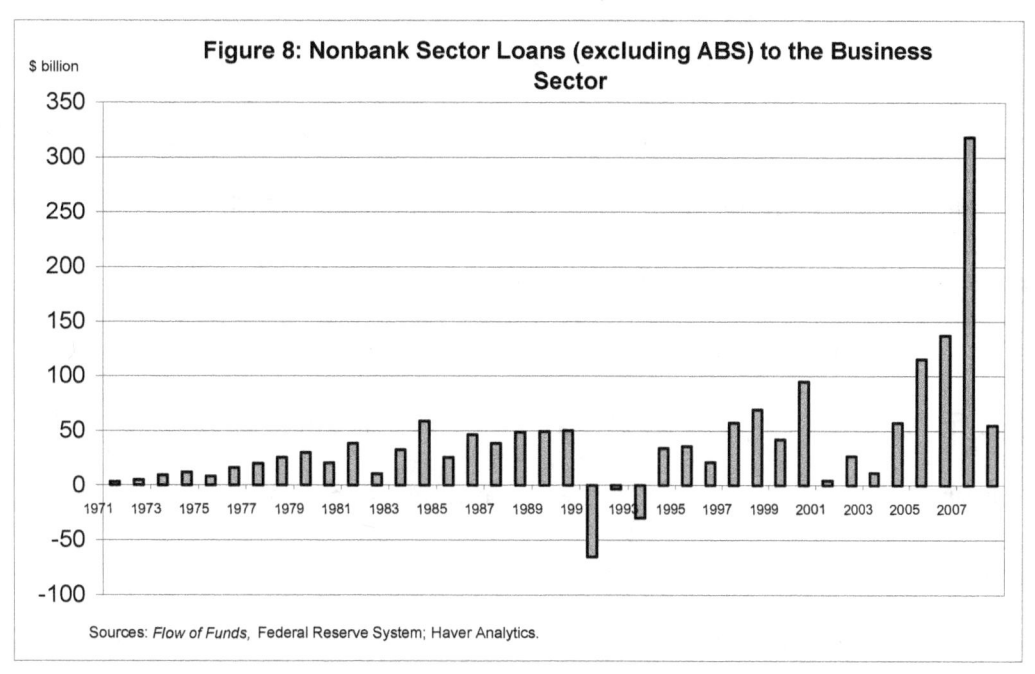

Figure 8: Nonbank Sector Loans (excluding ABS) to the Business Sector

Sources: *Flow of Funds,* Federal Reserve System; Haver Analytics.

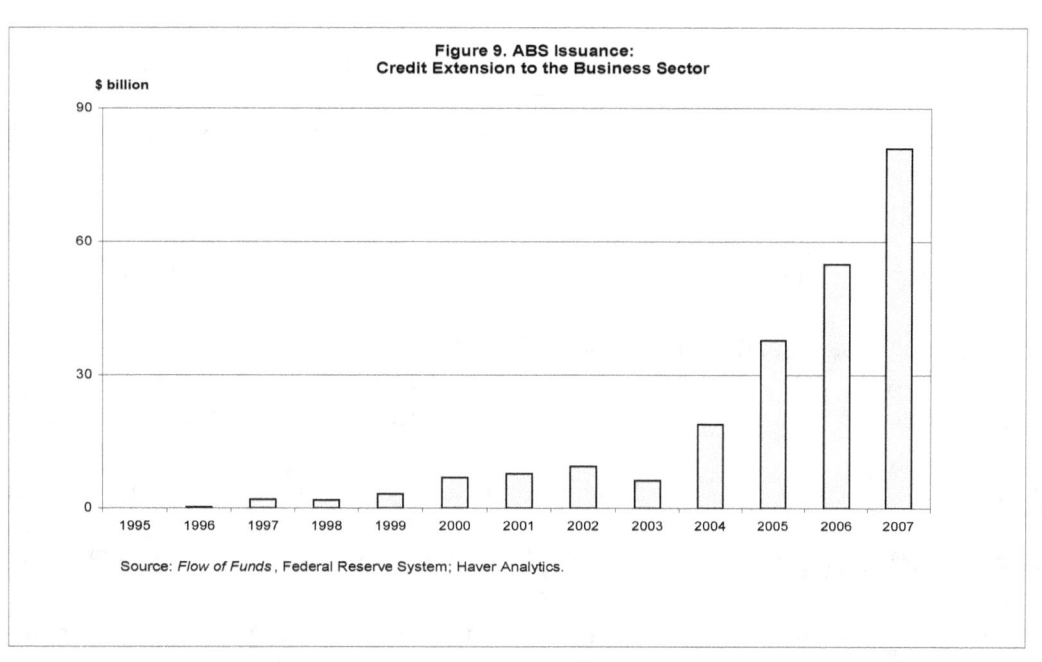

**Figure 9. ABS Issuance:
Credit Extension to the Business Sector**

Source: *Flow of Funds* , Federal Reserve System; Haver Analytics.

V.B. Other Scenarios for Financing Business Credit Needs in 2011

V.B.1. A Moribund Commercial Paper Market?

Suppose financing patterns do not converge to the baseline, Scenario 1 level: "Which shortfalls could be accommodated and which would be problematic?" Scenario 2 in Table 9 considers the case where the commercial paper market does not rebound to the relatively modest level outlined in Scenario 1. Could we expect banks and other credit providers to pick up the slack? Specifically, could they cover a shortfall of $25 billion in new commercial paper sales?

Scenario 2 in Table 9 shows the "stressed" element, commercial paper, in the cross-hatched cell. If businesses are unable to place any new commercial paper in the market, could banks take on an additional $10 billion of that shortfall, with other credit sources providing the remaining $15 billion? If banks preserve their long-run pattern of net new asset aquisition across asset categories, including in particular business nonmortgage loans, they would have to increase total net new asset aquisition from $1,100 billion to $1,150 billion, as shown in Scenario 2 (see the light gray cell in the second column of row 2). That level, while higher than the baseline so deemed stretched on the table, appears feasible as it amounts to less than a 5 percent "overshoot" from the projected baseline growth in bank balance sheets. It seems reasonable to expect that other credit sources could fund the remaining $15 billion shortfall. Bond buyers, most notably institutional bond investors, appear to have ample scope to increase bond purchases beyond our baseline assumption given the history of their bond purchase levels. Thus, Scenario 2 shows bond purchases increasing by $15 billion, thereby with banks supplying the total $25 billion commercial paper shortfall. As will be seen below, however, "other lenders" rather than bond buyers also have room to increase business credit provisioning, so other financing splits could make up for a moribund commercial paper market.

Scenario 3 takes the issue of a possible shortfall in the commercial paper market further, examining the extent to which a collapse in that market could be offset by business credit extension elsewhere. Row 3 (the cross-hatched cell in the commercial paper column) postulates a large net drop in commercial paper placement of $160 billion if the commercial paper market were unable to roll over any of its existing nonfinancial corporate outstanding liabilities. Could other business sector credit providers be expected to make up for the $160 billion roll-over failure, plus the $25 billion shortfall in baseline commercial paper issuance?

We could at this point consider whether the erstwhile investors in commercial paper might turn to some other investment vehicles which would still ultimately lead to their funding of U.S. nonfinancial business credit demand. But to foreshadow our analysis in the following paragraph, we do not need to address this issue because we find adequate funding for business credit demand in the absence of a functioning commercial paper market without reliance on the rechanneling of former commercial paper investment funds.

We assume that banks will again make up $10 billion of the commercial paper deficit. We turn to the bond market to make up $145 billion and other lenders to take up $30 billion of the remaining $175 billion deficit. Under the "Total" column in the "Bond Sales" section (the dotted cell), the $460 billion in bond sales is the result of the $145 billion increase. Would bond purchasers buy this additional amount? Such an expectation is in line with long-run corporate bond purchase patterns of institutional investors, private entities, and foreign buyers shown in row 3 in Table 9 (see the light gray cells under "Bond Sales"). Such purchase levels would be consistent with recent, fairly stable institutional investor purchases, while still well below recent private entity purchases and in line with recent foreign purchase amounts. (We've marked the levels of bond purchases under this scenario as stretched but feasible on Table 9 because they assume recent purchase levels would be maintained by important investor groups despite the financial crisis.) As for other lenders, an increase in loans to $90 billion would be in keeping with recent credit provision by these relatively steady lenders (again we mark this as a stretch but feasible outcome on Table 9 because it assumes recent behavior continues).

V.B.2. Anemic Corporate Bond Market Activity?

Few worry that the corporate bond market will be a net negative source of new business credit, but some observers are concerned with the possibility of a somewhat disrupted bond market. Scenario 4 considers whether other credit providers could compensate for a substantial fall off in corporate bond financing. That scenario posits a $65 billion decline in net new corporate bond sales overall (i.e., bond sales of $250 billion versus the $315 billion baseline), with an across-the-board drop in sales to nonbank investors. Table 9 shows a $35 billion drop in institutional investor bond appetite relative to baseline levels, a $5 billion drop in sales to private entities, and a $20 billion drop in foreign purchases of U.S. corporate bonds (see the cross-hatched cells in row 4). Banks are also assumed to cut bond demand by $5 billion. Of course, other combinations of pullback from bond purchases are possible. Could lending from other sources replace the approximately 20 percent slide in overall bond financing projected in Scenario 4?

An initial question to ask in this analysis is where does the investment money go that is now no longer being used to purchase U.S. nonfinancial corporate bonds. Could it find its way to funding the U.S. corporate sector through some other channel? Since bond investors by definition show a preference for holding tradable securities, it is unlikely they would view bank accounts as a satisfactory alternative investment without a significant rise in deposit interest rates. More likely, the erstwhile bond investors would switch to purchases of foreign bonds, government securities, or GSE securities. Consequently, we look to see if the other traditional sources of business credit could fill the bond funding gap in the absence of significant new funds flowing into these sources.

As established under Scenario 3, banks could increase net new business loans by as much as $10 billion. For banks to increase business loans by significantly more, either bank balance sheets would have to grow to an implausibly large degree or banks would have to divert funds from other credit demands. If they do not, a $55 billion shortfall in business financing remains. We demonstrated the lack of meaningful upside potential for the commercial paper market; in any case, it is difficult to believe that the market for one type of business debt — short-term commercial paper — could be pumped up at the same time long-term debt sales wilted, absent some major change in maturity preferences. Given the real estate focus of the CMBS market, other lenders are the only other source to address the remaining $55 billion gap. Traditional investors might provide, perhaps, a $30 billion share of that total. That means ABS issuers would have to lend businesses an additional $25 billion over their baseline, a level that seems unrealistically optimistic in the face of what would be subdued investor activity. Hence, potential scenarios for the corporate bond market are not "symmetric" in the following sense: although meaningful above-baseline bond market activity could materialize as the economy recovers, were the bond market to wither somewhat, either (1) business credit will be significantly crimped or (2) credit elsewhere will be crimped if banks diverted funds to business lending. In any event the cost of business credit would likely sharply rise.

Scenario 5 once again posits baseline bond market financing, but asks whether bank bond purchases could be expected to make up for an across-the-board drop in nonbanks' investment in corporate bonds such as described in Scenario 4 (i.e., the "stressed" cross-hatched cells in both scenarios show the same drop in nonbanks bond purchases). In that case, banks would have to purchase $90 billion in bonds, more than three times their baseline level. Could banks absorb this level of investment in corporate bonds in order to maintain the same level of overall activity in the bond market? Under the assumption that banks strive to maintain their baseline mortgage, consumer, and business lending targets (as they must in order to maintain their overall role in supporting moderate growth for the economy), the answer is clearly "no." That higher level of bond purchases would result in an impossible ballooning of banks total net asset aquisition to $3,500 billion, as shown by the dark gray cell in Scenario 5, or alternatively a significant increase (from 5 percent to 15 percent) in the share of bonds in banks' portfolios.

V.B.3. How Important Are Nonbank Lenders and the CMBS Market?

Two final scenarios are, first, whether banks and bond purchasers could pick up a substantial shortfall in direct business lending by nonbanks; and second, how crucial the CMBS market is to business mortgage-related financing. Scenario 6 considers the first case. Suppose other lenders provide only two-thirds as much lending to business as they do in the baseline scenario, reducing their credit provision to $45 billion from $70 billion: how difficult would it be for banks and bond purchasers to address the $25 billion shortfall? We show other lender credit in Scenario 6 (the cross-hatched "stressed" cells), broken down by traditional investors and ABS issuers. A pullback in nonbank lending is likely to be reflected mainly in reduced lending from traditional investors, given the already low level of ABS issuance in the baseline scenario. Correspondingly, this stress scenario has traditional investor credit falling by $20 billion and ABS issuance by $5 billion. In line with our earlier analysis, banks could increase lending by $10 billion, while an increase of $15 billion in bond sales appears readily attainable.[34] Thus, the role of other lenders does not appear to be critical to ensure an adequate level of business credit supply. Of note, a resuscitation of the ABS market in particular does not appear critical to business financing.

Banks' mortgage-related lending would have to make up any shortfall in the CMBS market, given that other credit providers focus on nonmortgage-related credit provision to businesses.[35] The current near-shutdown in the CMBS market (see Box 1 at the end of this paper) has concerned market participants and policymakers; its reemergence might be quite tepid, a possibility we have suggested could be represented with, say, a level similar to the CMBS market's 1990s–early-2000s level. Could banks' mortgage-related lending fill that gap? If banks allocated only the historical share of their balance sheet growth to commercial mortgage financing, their net asset aquisition would rise to $1,350 billion, almost 25 percent above the $1,100 billion baseline level. We consider that to be overly optimistic. Given recent problems in commercial mortgages, moreover, we would not anticipate banks diverting credit to this sector away from other credit areas without a sharp change in interest rates. Under these circumstances, commercial mortgage availability would likely be curtailed.

VI. Summary and Conclusions

Policymakers and financial market participants are focused intensely on stabilizing banking and financial markets during a period of unprecedented challenges. Nevertheless, it is not too soon to consider what the financial market landscape could look like once the turmoil

---

[34] This analysis would not be conceptually different if banks split the increase of $10 billion between lending and bond purchases.

[35] Institutional investors financed a substantial share of commercial mortgages before the CMBS market took root in the 1990s. These institutional investors no longer supply a significant share of commercial mortgages and are unlikely to be able to gear up quickly to reenter this area even if they chose to do so.

subsides and the economy has begun to recover. We suggest in this paper that 2011 is a reasonable horizon to consider. Our starting point is $16 trillion nominal GDP in 2011; our methodology could be adjusted easily to accommodate a higher, more optimistic level of economic growth, or a lower, more pessimistic forecast. We make use of the *Flow of Funds* data in a straightforward way, focusing on the net ***new level of credit extension*** activity that would have to arise to support private sector borrowing consistent with a return to trend level of nominal GDP and normal credit costs. We set aside the 2001–2008 bubble-to-bust time period, and instead use pre-2001 conditions as approximations of long-run behavior patterns in private sector credit extension. The mix of sources supplying credit for the home mortgage, consumer, and nonfinancial business sector markets is different, and so we consider each of those markets separately.

A common thread for all three markets is the role of banks. Banks play multiple direct and indirect roles in credit provision. Direct access to capital markets comes into play both in the sale of corporate bonds and commercial paper, and other, nonbank, lenders play a role in credit provision, as do traditional investors, including foreigners; the roles of each of these actors are addressed. Our focus is drawn to structured finance, specifically the GSE MBS market, (nonmortgage) consumer ABS issuers, and the CMBS market. Each of these sources of private sector credit provision raises fundamental questions about what to expect, especially as we consider how one or more of them might address shortfalls in credit provision by other actors. We posit a baseline scenario under which banks (on a broad definition, to take account of the recent absorption of large thrifts into the commercial banking industry) return to their long-run trend level of financing for home mortgage, consumer, and business sector borrowing.

Our key findings can be summarized as follows:

- The revival of structured finance is critical across all three sectors if credit availability and credit costs are to remain at acceptable levels without significant structural adjustments in credit markets. In the home mortgage market, the GSEs must sell enough MBS to support about half of borrowers' credit needs or mortgage rates will likely surge.[36] In addition, even if the GSEs provided more than half of all home mortgage credit (55 percent in our example), banks could not make up for the complete absence of private label securitizers, unless banks substantially cut back credit provision for nonmortgage consumer borrowing and/or business borrowing while raising mortgage interest rates. At least a modest role for private label MBS issuance in, for example, securitizing high-quality jumbo mortgage loans is likely necessary to ensure adequate mortgage credit availability at a normal interest cost.

- For consumer borrowing, without a substantial revival of the ABS market, banks and nonbank credit providers are unlikely to easily make up for the resultant shortfall. It is impossible to tell how rapid and significant renewed investor interest would be in securitized consumer loans; our analysis suggests that an ABS market recovery to at least half of its pre-crisis share of the provision of consumer credit is necessary for adequate consumer credit availability without other dislocation.

- For business sector credit, the reemergence of the CMBS market is essential for adequate provision of commercial mortgage credit at a reasonable cost; banks would likely be unwilling to fully make up for a large shortfall of CMBS-supported business sector credit without a very sharp price adjustment to this credit. In contrast, although the commercial paper market has traditionally played a role in business sector credit extension, banks and other credit channels likely could replace a credit shortfall resulting from a moribund commercial paper market without much price adjustment. In the corporate bond market, it is reasonable to expect at least a return to, and perhaps even an increase over, pre-boom financing trends. However, banks and other credit providers are unlikely to overcome a substantial shortfall in financing by way of the bond market if it were to occur.

In our view, these findings generate several important policy implications. First, in light of the need for moderate growth in bank credit extension through 2011, policymakers are well advised to focus on stabilizing bank capital and other elements underlying future credit extension. Second, any program to revamp the GSEs must be mindful of the dominant role that

---

[36] If there were to be a cutback in the supply of GSE MBS, investors likely would switch preferences to liquid government securities. Assuming no change in the supply of government securities to such increased demand by investors, there would likely be a sharp adjustment in relative interest rates, with mortgage and other interest rates rising relative to interest rates on government securities.

these entities are likely to continue to play in the mortgage market. Finally, a modest revival (at least) of structured finance appears extremely important in both the consumer credit market and the business sector credit market; hence, any policy measures that detract from that process risk generating a credit crunch in one or both markets.

References

Bank for International Settlements (2009). *79th Annual Report* (June 29).

Barth, James R., Tong Li, Wenling Lu, Triphon Phumiwasana, and Glenn Yago (2009). *The Rise and Fall of the U.S. Mortgage and Credit Markets.* John Wiley & Sons, Inc. Hoboken, N.J.

Congressional Budget Office (2009). *The Budget and Economic Outlook: Fiscal Years 2009 to 2019* (January). Congress of the United States, Washington, D.C.

Department of the Treasury (2009). *Financial Regulatory Reform: A New Foundation,* (June). Washington, D.C.

FitchRatings (2009). "Off-Balance Sheet Accounting Changes: SFAS 166 and SFAS 167," *Financial Institutions U.S.A. Special Report* (June 22).

LaMonte, Mark (2009). "Moody's Credit Card Statement," *Moody's Investor Service, Special Edition* (June 16) p. 4.

Levine, Ross (2005). "Finance and Growth: Theory and Evidence." In Phillippe Aghion and Stephen Durlauf (eds.), *Handbook of Economic Growth.* The Netherlands: Elsevier Science.

Nolle, Daniel E. (2009). "What is different about this recession? Nonbank providers of credit loom large," In *Quarterly CPP Evaluation Report*, Office of Financial Stability, Department of the Treasury (August 17). http://financialstability.gov/impact/ CPPreport.html.

U.S. General Accountability Office (2009). *Financial Markets Regulation: Financial Crisis Highlights Need to Improve Oversight of Leverage at Financial Institutions and Across System*, GAO-09-739 (July 22). Washington, D.C.

Box 1: Changing Nature of Credit Extension in the U.S. Economy[a]

As economists and policymakers begin identifying and analyzing the causes of the ongoing financial crisis, attention has naturally focused on the banking system.[b] Nevertheless, industry experts are aware that nonbank entities play an increasingly important role in finance and merit consideration from an analytic and a policymaking point of view. Indeed, a consensus has begun to emerge that the current condition of some components of the so-called "shadow banking system" may present particularly challenging obstacles to the reestablishment of financial market stability. Thus, a brief overview of the major players in the credit provision system is in order, with special emphasis on major credit provision "bottlenecks" in structured finance markets.

Figure A1 uses *Flow of Funds* data to divide credit providers into three broad groups: (1) "banks," composed of broadly similar depository institutions (operating under similar regulatory regimes), including commercial banks, bank holding companies, thrifts, and credit unions; (2) nonbanks providing credit via "structured finance" (that is, mortgage-backed securities and other asset-backed securities); and (3) all other nonbank credit providers. There is no single definition of the shadow banking system, but one way to think of it is as the combination of the latter two groups. Figure A1 shows trends in the shares of outstanding balances of debt held by, or credit extended by, each of these three broad groups, going back almost four decades.

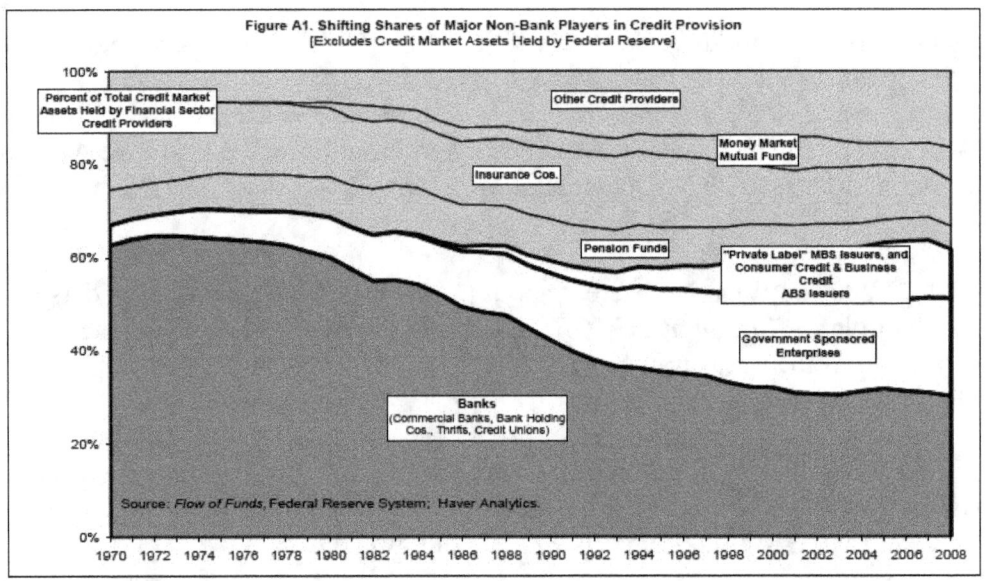

The financial sector traditionally holds about three-fourths of all credit market assets, which corresponds to three-fourths of credit market debt owed across the economy. (The two other sectors holding credit market assets are domestic nonfinancial providers and foreigners.) Figure A1 shows that the share of credit extended by banks was halved over the period, declining from more than 60 percent in 1970 to about 30 percent by the end of 2008. Figure A1 also shows that structured finance greatly increased in relative importance, growing from 4 percent of credit provision in 1970 to more than 30 percent by the end of 2008. That growth was largely at the expense of the banking sector's on-balance-sheet share of credit provision, and by 2008 — as the current financial crisis blossomed — all three major groups of credit providers had approximately the same relative importance across the economy.

---

[a] The discussion in Box 1 draws heavily on that in Nolle (2009) (http://financialstability.gov/impact/ CPPreport html).

[b] For an outline of the major events of and policy responses to the ongoing financial and economic crisis see *Financial Turmoil Timeline* (http:/www newyorkfed.org/research/global_economy/Crisis_Timeline.pdf), Federal Reserve Bank of New York.

[Box 1 continued]

Turning from credit extension balances outstanding to the flow of (net) new credit, figure A2 illustrates the abrupt plunge in credit flows from both the banking sector and structured finance sector in 2008 as the crisis took hold, after strong increases in the provision of credit by both sectors over the 2001–2007 bubble period. (The upward surge in credit provision in 2008 by "all other nonbank providers" was largely a consequence of Federal Reserve System funding of the commercial paper market at the end of the third quarter and during the fourth quarter.)

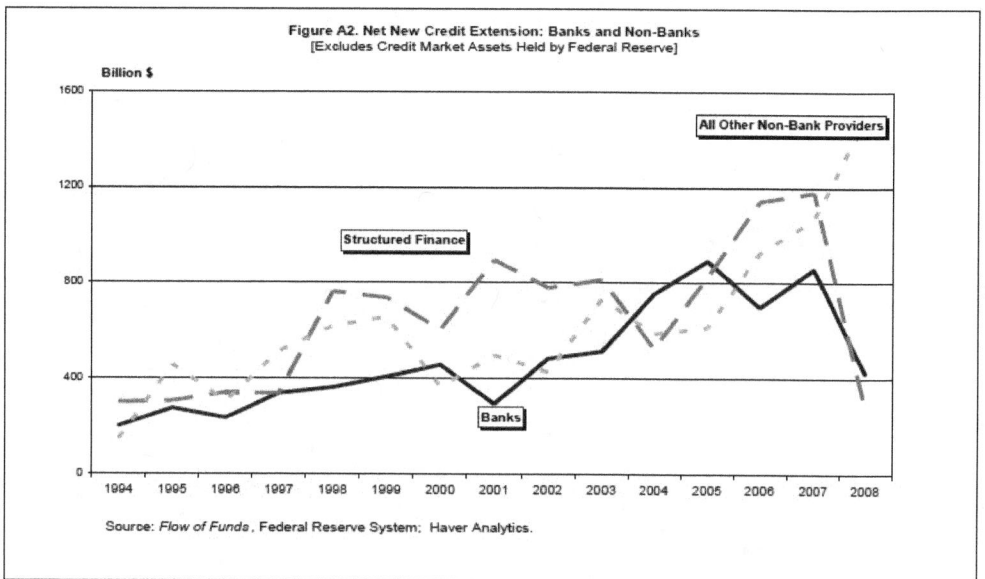

The plunge in credit provision by the structured finance market varied across players in those markets. Figure A3 looks at the MBS market, focusing on GSE and private label MBS issuance from the beginning of 2008 through July 2009. (The new issuance data in figure A3 are somewhat different from those in figure A2, which shows *net credit flows* — that is, inflows *minus* reductions.) The most salient development in the MBS market is that there is almost no private label issuance.

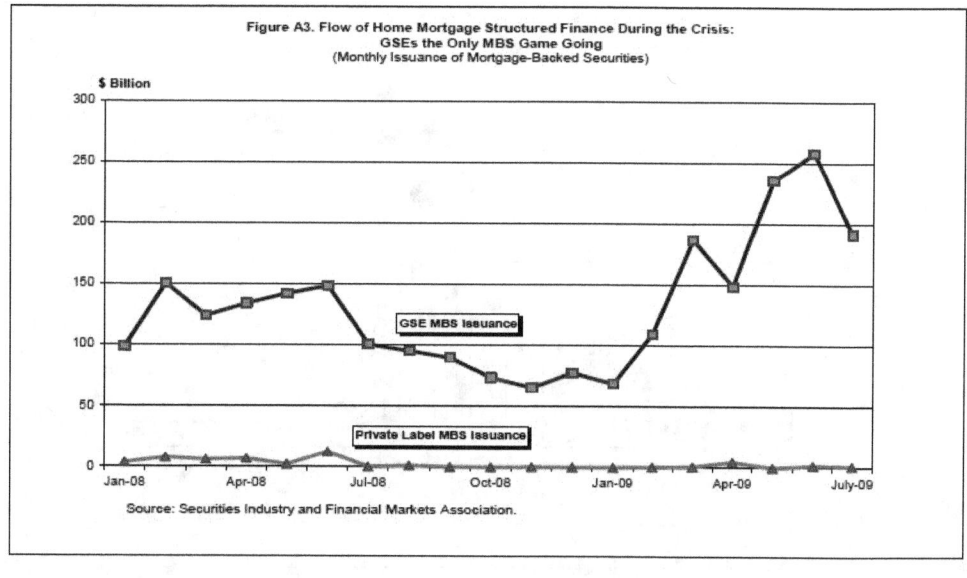

[Box 1 continued]

There is also a large credit provision "hole" caused by the plunge in consumer ABS issuance. Figure A4 illustrates the precipitous drop in issuance in 2008 in three large components of the consumer ABS market, and the so-far anemic recovery in those components. Credit card ABS issuance fell from almost $30 billion at the beginning of 2008 to virtually zero at by the end of that year; the recovery in second quarter of 2009 suggests that some progress has been made. Similar patterns hold in the auto and student loan ABS markets.

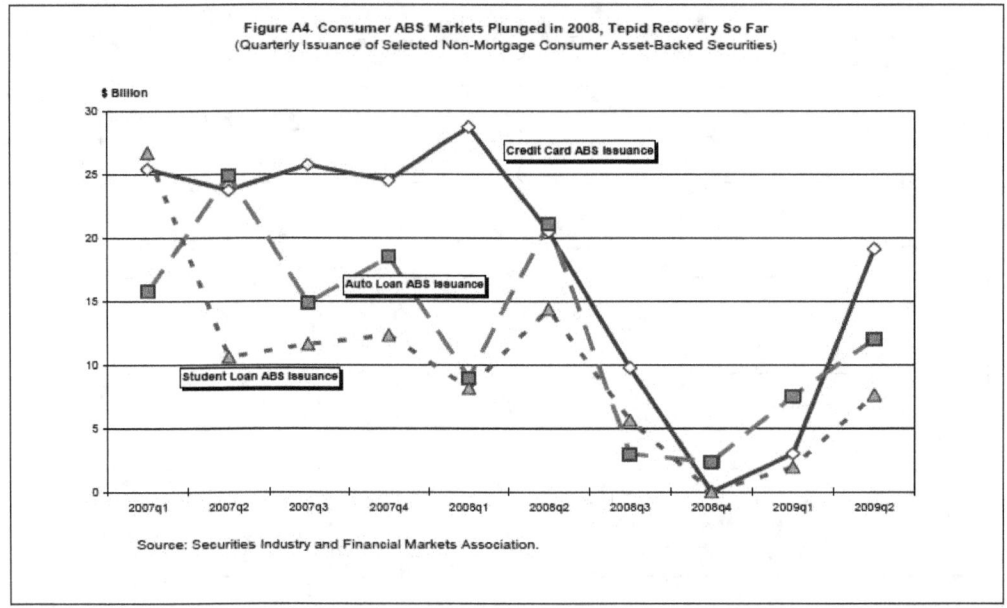

As serious as the downturn in consumer ABS market has been, conditions in the market for commercial mortgage-backed securities (CMBS) appeared worse as of part way through Q2 2009. Figure A5 shows that as of May 2009, both U.S. and non-U.S. CMBS markets were completely shut down.

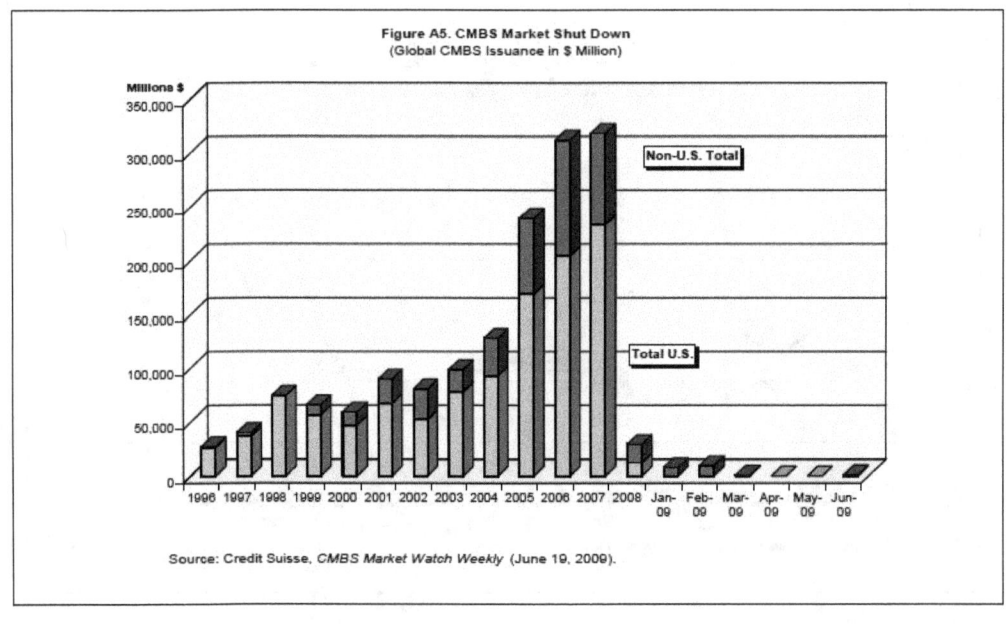

Box 2. Interrelationship between Banks and Structured Finance

The relationship between the banking sector and the structured finance sector is complicated. This is especially true in the provision of home mortgage credit and credit card loans. Figure A6 illustrates part of the mortgage-market complexity of the bank-structured finance interrelationship using year-end data from banks' Consolidated Reports of Condition and Income ("call reports"). The bottom portion of each bar shows home mortgage loans held on banks' balance sheets, while the top portion of each bar shows the value of home mortgage loans that banks sold into the securitization process.[a] Because of this "originate-to-distribute" activity, some argue that analyses may "undercount" banks' role in the mortgage market. But banks also purchase MBS, a fact reflected in the middle portion of each bar in Figure A6 showing the value of mortgage-backed securities in which banks have invested. In effect, banks have indirectly provided mortgage financing in this amount, through the structured finance markets. Another way to think about this is to note that, because both the bottom (dark gray) and middle (white) portion of the bars in Figure A6 are on-balance-sheet mortgage credit extension activities of banks, they are captured in the bottom "Bank" segment of Figure A1 (Box 1), while the top (light gray) portion of the bars in Figure A6 is mortgage credit extension captured in the structured finance (middle) portion of Figure A1. Figure A6 shows that banks' investments in MBS has routinely been greater than the value of the mortgage loans they originate and then sell off; in effect, banks as a group make investments in mortgage credit in excess of what they "originate-and-distribute." Viewed in this light, it is difficult to argue that the *Flow of Funds* necessarily underestimates banks' role in mortgage credit extension.

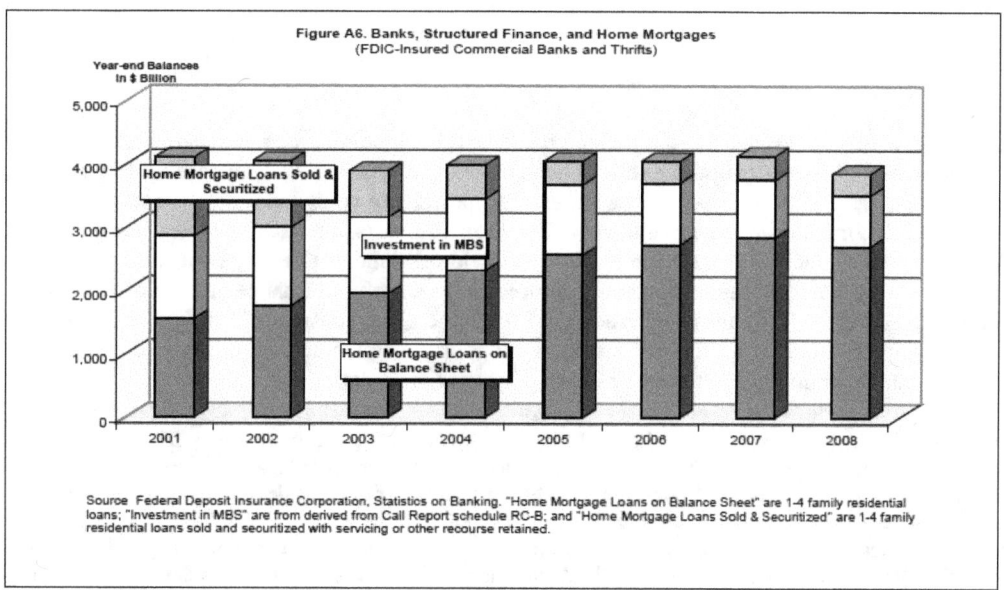

Figure A6. Banks, Structured Finance, and Home Mortgages
(FDIC-Insured Commercial Banks and Thrifts)

Source: Federal Deposit Insurance Corporation, Statistics on Banking. "Home Mortgage Loans on Balance Sheet" are 1-4 family residential loans; "Investment in MBS" are from derived from Call Report schedule RC-B; and "Home Mortgage Loans Sold & Securitized" are 1-4 family residential loans sold and securitized with servicing or other recourse retained.

The bank-structured finance interconnection also extends to consumer credit provision. This is especially true in the credit card market. In particular, as Figure A7 illustrates, banks dominate credit card ABS issuance, accounting for between 65 percent and 85 percent of total issuance over 2002-2008. By comparison, banks have a far smaller presence in other consumer ABS issuance, including those based on pools of auto loans and student loans.[b]

---

[a] As noted at the bottom of Figure A6, the mortgage loans sold were securitized with servicing or other recourse retained; i.e., banks still retained some measure of responsibility for the performance of those loans. Loans sold but not securitized are not included in that component. Note that the data in Figure A6 is for commercial banks and thrifts.

[b] For example, over the past two years (2007 and 2008), banks' direct involvement in auto loan ABS issuance never reached more than 15 percent of the market in any given month, and in some periods was 0 percent (Deutsche Bank, *Securitzation Monthly* (various issues)). Banks' direct issuance of student loan ABS has also been minimal.

[Box 2 continued]

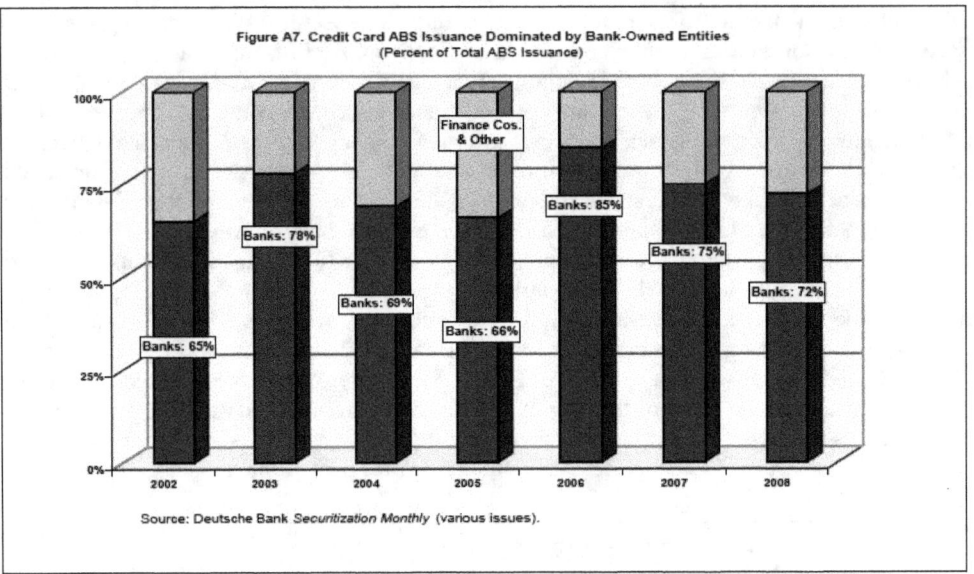

Figure A7. Credit Card ABS Issuance Dominated by Bank-Owned Entities
(Percent of Total ABS Issuance)

Source: Deutsche Bank *Securitization Monthly* (various issues).

ABS issuance is an off-balance-sheet activity, which banks and bank holding companies undertake in ABS-issuing trusts known as "qualified special purpose entities" (also called "QSPEs" or "Qs"). These QSPEs are generally wholly owned subsidiaries of credit card issuing banks or bank holding companies, and as such fall under the banking system regulation and supervision umbrella. For *Flow of Funds* purposes however, because the pools of credit card loans on which such ABS issuance is based are held off-balance sheet by banks, they are not included in the "Banks" portion of Figure A1, and instead are captured in the structured finance portion of that figure.[c] As with the MBS market, banks include purchases of credit card ABS and other consumer (and business) credit ABS in their securities portfolios on-balance sheet; these investments, supporting consumer and business credit extension, are included in the "Banks" portion of Figure A1 based on *Flow of Funds* data.

---

[c] The impending implementation of new financial accounting standards under FAS 140 in January 2010 would change this to some extent. Under the new guidelines, the pools of credit card loans (and other pooled loans) sold by the bank to its QSPE (qualified special purpose entity) would be brought back on balance sheet. This asset-side transaction would be matched by on-boarding to the liabilities side of the balance sheet the funding from sales of the credit card (and other) ABS. For the banking industry and some market observers and participants, the key issue is not the on-boarding of currently off-balance-sheet assets therefore, but rather the fact that bringing these assets back on-balance sheet necessarily requires the bank to increase capital in proportion to the risk-weighting assigned to the assets.